ANIMALS
OF THE WORLD

Authors: Martin Walters and Jinny Johnson

Editor: Steve Parker

Consultant Editor: Brian Williams

This edition designed by Starry Dog Books.

This is a Parragon book
This edition published in 2006

Parragon
Queen Street House
4 Queen Street
Bath BA1 1HE, UK

British Library Cataloguing-in-Publication Data

A catalogue record for this book is available from the British Library.

ISBN 1-40546-935-8

ANIMALS
OF THE WORLD

p

A WORLD
FULL OF
ANIMALS
6

SIMPLE
ANIMALS
10

THE MICROWORLD
OF PROTISTS   12

MOSS ANIMALS   14

SPONGES   16

JELLYFISH   18

ANEMONES AND
PARTNERS   20

CORALS   22

WORMS, SNAILS
& STARFISH
24

EARTHWORMS AND LEECHES
26

BRISTLEWORMS   28

THE RANGE OF
MOLLUSCS   30

SLUGS AND SNAILS   32

SQUID, OCTOPUSES AND
CUTTLEFISH   34

STARFISH AND
SEASTARS   36

INSECTS &
OTHER
ARTHROPODS
38

THE WORLD OF BUGS   40

BEETLES AND WEEVILS   42

BUTTERFLIES AND MOTHS
44

CRICKETS AND
GRASSHOPPERS   46

CRABS, LOBSTERS
AND SHRIMPS   48

SPIDERS   50

FISH
52

WHAT ARE FISH?   54

SHARKS AND RAYS   56

CHARACINS, CARP AND
CATFISH   58

SCORPIONFISH AND
SEAHORSES   60

FLATFISH AND TRIGGERFISH
62

PERCH, GROUPERS
AND DRUMS   64

AMPHIBIANS & REPTILES
66

WHAT ARE AMPHIBIANS? 68

FROGS AND TOADS 70

WHAT ARE REPTILES? 72

TORTOISES, TURTLES AND TERRAPINS 74

CROCODILES AND ALLIGATORS 76

IGUANAS, AGAMIDS AND CHAMELEONS 78

PYTHONS, BOAS AND THREAD SNAKES 80

BIRDS
82

FLIGHTLESS BIRDS 84

SEABIRDS 86

HERONS, DUCKS AND GEESE 88

BIRDS OF PREY 90

PIGEONS, DOVES AND PARROTS 92

OWLS AND NIGHTJARS 94

CROWS, SHRIKES AND BOWERBIRDS 96

SPARROWS, FINCHES AND WEAVERS 98

MAMMALS
100

EGG-LAYING MAMMALS 102

MARSUPIAL MAMMALS 104

BATS 106

ANTEATERS, SLOTHS AND ARMADILLOS 108

RABBITS, HARES AND PIKAS 110

MICE, RATS AND CAVIES 112

LARGE RODENTS 114

DEER, CAMELS AND PIGS 116

HORSES, ZEBRAS AND RHINOS 118

ELEPHANTS 120

CATS 122

DOGS, FOXES AND HYENAS 124

BEARS, RACCOONS AND PANDAS 126

SEALS, SEA LIONS AND SEA COWS 128

GREAT WHALES 130

DOLPHINS AND PORPOISES 132

ORANGS AND GORILLAS 134

CHIMPANZEES 136

GLOSSARY 138
INDEX 140
ACKNOWLEDGEMENTS 144

A WORLD FULL OF ANIMALS

◭ Boa constrictor

The world teems with animals. Almost everywhere we look, creatures are going about their daily lives. On a walk through the countryside we see birds high in the sky. Insects buzz around the flowers. Mice and voles scamper through the undergrowth. Rabbits race across fields. Worms burrow in the soil under our feet. Even in a busy city, pigeons flock and cockroaches scuttle.

These are a tiny selection of the kinds of animals that live on Earth. No one is sure exactly how many there are. Nearly two million kinds, or species, have been studied and identified by scientists. But many remote mountains, rainforests, coastlines and deep seas

◭ Mushroom

remain to be explored. The total number of animal species on Earth may be 10 million, 20 million or even more. Most of them are likely to be small insects such as beetles.

THE KINGDOMS OF LIVING THINGS

Scientists used to divide the living world into two main groups, or kingdoms: plants and animals. Today, most experts agree that there are five kingdoms. Two consist of microscopic life-forms, where each individual is just one living cell. One of these kingdoms is Monerans, including the germs known as bacteria.

◭ Manta ray

The other kingdom is Protists. Some protists are like tiny, one-celled micro-animals. They move about and eat food. So they are included at the beginning of this book (pages 12–13). The third kingdom is Plants, such as flowers, trees, grasses, ferns and seaweeds; and the fourth is Fungi, such as mushrooms, toadstools and yeasts. The fifth kingdom, and the largest, is the Animals.

WHAT ARE ANIMALS?

Animals are multi-celled living things that get the energy they need for survival, and the nutrients they need for growth and repair, by feeding on other living things.

◭ Wild bees

EVOLUTION

Evolution is when living things change or adapt to their surroundings. The world is always changing, as weather and climate alter, seas rise and fall, volcanoes erupt and earthquakes split the land. Living things change too, developing new bodily features and behaviour, so they can survive better in the new and different conditions. But survival is a continuing struggle. It is as if nature chooses or selects which plants and animals will survive, and which will die. This is evolution by natural selection.

Evolution has been happening since life first appeared on Earth some 4 billion years ago. It has meant that some kinds of animals have died out, or become extinct, while others have evolved to take their place. All of this usually happens over a very long time scale, thousands or millions of years. But we have altered the world greatly in the last few hundred years. New types of living things can now be produced in a few weeks or months using the science of genetics. How this will affect nature in the future is very unclear.

◭ Tuatara

⬥ Caterpillars

In this way they differ from plants, which capture their energy from sunlight.

Most animals feed by eating or ingesting their food. Carnivores such as wolves eat meat. Herbivores like deer feed on plant parts. Detritivores like worms and millipedes feed on dead and rotting bits of other living things. Omnivores eat almost anything.

Some, such as mammals, certain snakes and some fish, give birth to babies. A few, such as some flatworms, starfish and jellyfish, can split and grow into two new individuals.

Animals care for their offspring in different ways. Monkeys and apes look after their babies for months, or even years. Most birds spend weeks tirelessly feeding the chicks that hatch from their eggs. Mouth-brooding fish shelter their young in their mouths. The gastric-brooding frog keeps its young tadpoles in its stomach! However, most animals lay or release their eggs, and have nothing more to do with the offspring.

Most animals have sense organs such as eyes and ears, so they can detect changes around them. They also have muscles so they can move about, react to changes, find food and avoid danger. However, very simple animals like sponges have few senses and cannot move. Some animals, like mussels and barnacles, fix themselves into position when young and stay put for the rest of their lives.

HOW ANIMALS BREED
The key feature of all living things is that they breed – they produce more of their kind. Animals do this in a huge variety of ways. Many, from butterflies to birds, lay eggs.

⬥ Horned grebe

⬥ Puffin

7

Animals live in almost every type of surroundings, or habitat. A waterless desert, an icy glacier, a wave-battered coastline, a deep and pitch-black cave – they are all homes to animals of one kind or another. Each type of animal has features that enable it to survive in its habitat. Glacier grasshoppers can be frozen alive, yet come back to life when thawed out. Desert creatures escape the drought and heat by burrowing underground and staying still or dormant until it rains once more.

⬛ Shrimp on a sea slug

HARMFUL, HELPFUL AND USEFUL

Some animals have taken to living alongside people. We have covered much of the world with buildings, roads, factories and rubbish tips. These have become ideal habitats for animals such as cockroaches, rats, mice and gulls. Some animals have become pests. Insects feed on cereal grains and destroy our crops. Some creatures, like flukes and mosquitoes, cause or spread disease.

But we have also found other animals helpful or useful. We have bred farm animals for meat, milk, fur and skins. Working animals pull ploughs and carts or carry goods. Horses, dogs, camels, falcons, frogs and others are used in sports and competitions. For some people, pets are their main companions.

EQUAL ANIMALS

When we talk about "animals and birds", some people think of furry mammals and fluffy chicks. But the animal kingdom contains a gigantic range of creatures – including insects, spiders, snakes, worms, slugs, snails and other less appealing "creepy-crawlies". We may not want to pick them up, but they each have their role to play in nature.

Today, many animal species are in danger of extinction, due to our human activities.

⬛ Frogs

⬛ Stinkbug

⬛ Penguins and chicks

⬛ Young male lion

GROUPING ANIMALS

To study and understand the animal kingdom, we need to have some method of grouping or classifying its creatures. Those with important similarities are put together in the same group. The main division is between vertebrates and invertebrates.

🔺 Hagfish

Vertebrates are animals with backbones and include fish, frogs and other amphibians, lizards and other reptiles, birds and furry mammals. Invertebrates lack a backbone and include all other animals, from tiny flies to giant squid. This book is organized into sections using the standard system of classifying animals. It begins with simple invertebrates such as sponges and jellyfish. It ends with mammals that have complex behaviour, such as solving problems and using tools. Classification panels give details of how many species are in the group, where they live, what they eat and other information.

The classification system is broadly based on the idea of evolution. For example, all birds are classified together in the group called Aves. They are probably all descended from very early birds that first evolved millions of years ago. So all birds are related to each other. On a wider scale, the first birds probably evolved from reptiles such as the dinosaurs. In this way, relationships spread throughout the animal kingdom.

🔻 Backswimmer

It is tempting to see this system as a "ladder of evolution", with simple animals at the bottom and apes, monkeys — and ourselves — at the top. But all animals have amazing adaptations. A penguin might not survive on its own in one of our large cities. But then, we would not survive on our own at the South Pole!

🔺 Sheep

We hunt them for "sport", kill them for collections and eliminate them in case they are dangerous. Most of all, we take over their wild places so they no longer have anywhere to live. Habitat destruction is the major threat facing the natural world today. Without these animals, our world would be a far less exciting place.

▶ Horned owl

9

▶The man-o'-war is a cnidarian
— or rather, lots of cnidarians. It is
a floating group of cnidarian
polyps known as siphonophores.

SECTION 1
SIMPLE ANIMALS

THE SIMPLEST OF ALL LIFE FORMS ARE NOT ANIMALS. They are protists. Each is just a single living cell. Some are like microanimals, because they eat tiny bits of food. Others are like microplants, using the sun's light energy to live and grow. Protists number untold trillions and are the basic food for many tiny animals, especially in the sea, where they form much of the plankton.

A simple animal is a creature with few uncomplicated body parts. The simplest of the life forms we call animals are sponges. Each is little more than a collection of fairly similar cells, with no brain, heart, muscles or similar body parts. Sponges live in rivers and lakes, and on seashores and ocean floors, around the world. Crawling and swimming among them are tiny animals smaller than pinheads, such as water-bears and wheel-animals. Floating above them in the sea are various creatures that resemble bags of jelly. They include comb jellies and jellyfish, all with long, stinging tentacles.

Close relatives of jellyfish are the sea anemones on the shore, and the anemones' similar but smaller cousins, coral polyps. All of these animals may have few and simple body parts. But they thrive in their millions. Indeed, coral polyps construct the largest animal-made structures on Earth – coral reefs.

THE MICROWORLD OF PROTISTS

PROTISTS ARE VERY SMALL. They are among the tiniest living things, and each is made of just one microscopic cell. An average protist is about 20 times smaller than the dot on this letter 'i'. A very large protist might fit into this letter 'o'. In the deep sea lives a gigantic kind of protist that grows to the size of your finger. Protists are living things, but they are not really animals or plants. They have a separate kingdom (major group) of their own, Protista. However, some kinds, called protozoans, are like tiny animals (rather than tiny plants) because they can move around and they eat other living things – especially other protists! They are found in all watery or damp places, including seas, rivers, ponds, soil and on and inside animals and plants. Some kinds cause diseases.

There are many different kinds of protists. Amoebas are shaped like blobs and they can move around by changing shape as they ooze along like plastic bags of jelly. An amoeba feeds by sending out arm-like parts to surround a micro-particle of food, and then merging the arms with its body to engulf the particle. After digesting what it can, the amoeba simply oozes on and leaves the remains behind.

PLASMODIUM AND MALARIA

The protists that cause malaria grow through many stages in their lives. Some are in mosquitoes, some in humans. When a mosquito that does not have plasmodia bites a person who does have them, the mosquito sucks up plasmodia in its meal of blood. Then it bites another person and passes on the parasites.

Plasmodia multiply inside mosquito

Plasmodia enter cells of person's liver

Plasmodia multiply inside liver cells

Mosquito bites person and passes plasmodium parasites into the blood

liver

Mosquito bites person with malaria and sucks up blood containing the plasmodia parasites

Plasmodia burst out of red blood cells into the blood

Plasmodia enter red blood cells and multiply inside them

Plasmodia burst out of liver cells and enter the blood stream

A few types of amoeba are real giants, growing almost to the size of shirt buttons.

Another group of protists is the ciliates, such as stentors and parameciums (pages 14–15). They are known as ciliates because their bodies are covered by a "carpet" of miniature hairs called cilia.

The cilia beat regularly, like rows of miniature oars, to make the protist glide through the water. However, some ciliates, like stentor, cannot move about. They are attached by a stalk to the pond or stream bottom. They beat their cilia to make water currents that bring tiny bits of food to them.

THE AMAZING SLIME MOULDS

Sometimes a slimy, slug-shaped blob appears on an old tree. It looks like jelly, but gradually, over several minutes, it moves! This is a slime mould. It is not a single creature, but a collection of hundreds of single-celled living things resembling amoebas. They normally live separately in the soil and among leaves. They gather together into a slug-like lump to breed. After creeping about for a while, the "slug" grows a stalk that releases tiny, dust-like particles called spores. These blow away and hatch into new amoebas. A large slime mould "slug" can weigh up to 900 g.

PROTISTS AND DISEASES

Many protists are parasites. They thrive on or in other living things, known as the hosts. The protist gains food and protection or shelter from its host. Some parasitic protists have hardly any effect on their hosts. Others cause great harm and serious diseases such as malaria and sleeping sickness. Malaria is common in many warm, tropical regions. The protists that cause it are known as plasmodia. They are spread by mosquitoes. When a mosquito bites a person, but before it sucks up blood, it passes a few thousand plasmodia protists into the person's body. These plasmodia parasites multiply inside the person's liver and blood. Eventually they produce the sweating, shivering, headaches and other symptoms of the disease malaria. People who visit tropical places where malaria is common can take tablets or have injections to prevent them catching it.

🅐 Protists come in many shapes. Some are almost perfect spheres, like these diatoms. Others are shaped like bananas or commas.

PROTIST PARTS

covering of cilia
oral groove (mouth)

stalk
holdfast

The protist called stentor is shaped like a microscopic mushroom. It lives in ponds, lakes and slow-flowing streams, fixed to something solid by its holdfast. Every now and again it comes loose and wriggles to a new place.

An amoeba is easily small enough to fit onto the head of a pin. It lives in water. It has no proper shape. It can spread out almost flat, extend arm-like parts called pseudopodia, then form into a round ball and roll along.

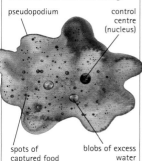

pseudopodium
control centre (nucleus)

spots of captured food
blobs of excess water

World Watch

PROTISTS

(Kingdom *Protista*)
• more than 60,000 kinds or species
• live in water, soil, other damp places and inside creatures and plants
• most are microscopic
• single-celled (body made of only one cell)

Some main groups of protists:

Amoebas
• 16,000 species
• move about and feed by changing shape
• some gather together and are known as "slime moulds"

Ciliates
• 7,500 species
• move and feed by tiny hair-like cilia

Euglenas
• at least 1,000 species
• mainly freshwater
• have one long, whip-like flagellum
• can capture the energy in sunlight, like tiny plants

Parasitic protists
• 5,000 species
• live inside other animals
• some cause diseases, such as malaria, sleeping sickness and dysentery

MOSS ANIMALS

MOSS ANIMALS OR BRYOZOANS, SOMETIMES CALLED SEA MOSSES, DO NOT LOOK LIKE ANIMALS AT ALL. As their name suggests, they live in the sea and look more like a patch of moss or a similar plant, or even like a doormat. This is because the tiny moss animals live together in a group or colony and extend their tentacles, like hundreds of miniature sea anemones. The tentacles wave in the water and filter floating bits of food, which the moss animals eat and digest.

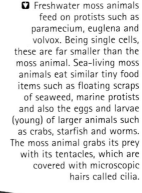

◘ Freshwater moss animals feed on protists such as paramecium, euglena and volvox. Being single cells, these are far smaller than the moss animal. Sea-living moss animals eat similar tiny food items such as floating scraps of seaweed, marine protists and also the eggs and larvae (young) of larger animals such as crabs, starfish and worms. The moss animal grabs its prey with its tentacles, which are covered with microscopic hairs called cilia.

Euglena

Paramecium

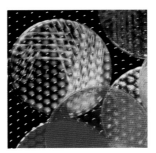

◄ Tiny creatures such as moss animals, and the one-celled protists, eat the smallest living things — especially bacteria. Some bacteria hardly seem alive. They can be dried out, boiled, frozen and even made into crystals in laboratory dishes (left). Yet they still become active when conditions are right.

In some ways, moss animals are similar to coral animals (page 22). Each one is tiny, only about half a pinhead across. It lives inside a hard, stony case and puts its tentacles into the water to catch floating pieces of food. Hundreds or thousands of individual moss animals are connected together into a flat, branching structure which spreads and grows over an underwater object. This object may be a rock or stone, a piece of wood, a large frond of seaweed, or even the shell of another animal like a clam or mussel. In some kinds of moss animal, the colony grows upwards, like a plant, rooted at the base to a firm object. The cases of neighbouring moss animals, known as zooids, are cemented to each other. The whole colony may widen like a fan or branch like a twig, and be brightly coloured. It can have millions of individuals, resembling a piece of coral. But most moss animals are less spectacular. They live in small, flat, pale-looking colonies, rarely larger than coins.

FRESHWATER MOSS ANIMALS

Most types of moss animal live in the sea, but a few live in fresh water, especially if it is clean and unpolluted.

INSIDE A MOSS ANIMAL

A typical moss animal or bryozoan is about the size of a pinhead. It lives in a hard casing, shaped like a shoebox, that it makes around itself from hard, chalky minerals taken from the water. The bell-shaped ring of feathery tentacles surrounding its mouth filter tiny particles of food, like small algae (plants) and protists, from the water. These food particles are passed down into the mouth and digested in the bag-like stomach. When danger threatens, strong strands of muscle pull the tentacles into the casing and then close and hold down the door-like lid, the operculum.

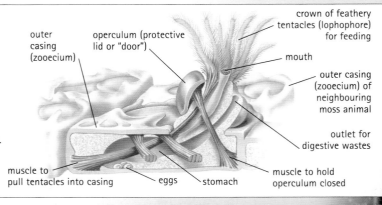

outer casing (zooecium)

operculum (protective lid or "door")

crown of feathery tentacles (lophophore) for feeding

mouth

outer casing (zooecium) of neighbouring moss animal

outlet for digestive wastes

muscle to pull tentacles into casing

eggs

stomach

muscle to hold operculum closed

In some kinds the protective case is flexible and jelly-like, rather than hard and stony. In the late summer or autumn, both sea and freshwater moss animal colonies produce hard, egg-like structures. These survive through the winter and can resist freezing and drying out. The eggs may blow about in the wind, spreading the moss animals to new places. In the spring they develop into new colonies.

SEA MAT AND HORNWRACK

The sea mat is one common kind of moss animal. It grows on the fronds of kelps and similar brown seaweeds and forms flat, pale, lacy sheets that stand out well against the background of the seaweed frond. Another common type of moss animal is called hornwrack. It grows about as long as a human hand and is found in deeper water along rocky coasts. Sometimes colonies of hornwrack are washed up on the shore after a storm, and they look like pieces of pale, lacy seaweed.

THE ANIMAL CELL

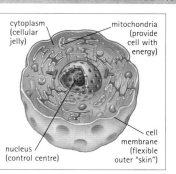

The bodies of all creatures, from moss animals to blue whales, are made of microscopic units known as cells. A typical animal cell is shown right. A protist is just one, all-purpose cell. A moss animal is about 5,000 cells. An elephant's body has 100 million million cells.

cytoplasm (cellular jelly)

mitochondria (provide cell with energy)

nucleus (control centre)

cell membrane (flexible outer "skin")

ENTOPROCTS

Entoprocts are another group of tiny creatures, very similar to moss animals. The largest are only as big as rice grains. They live mainly in colonies and are fixed in one spot. Some grow on stones, others on seaweeds. A few live on other animals, including sponges, worms, crabs and shellfish. Each entoproct has a horseshoe-shaped ring of about 40 tentacles for feeding, a cup-shaped body and a stalk fixing it to its host.

Moss animals
(Ectoprocts or Polyzoans)
• about 4,000 species
• aquatic (live in water)
• mostly marine or sea-dwelling
• grow as rooted, branching colonies
• each animal has a bell-shaped ring of tentacles called the lophophore, for feeding
• most individuals are hermaphrodite (have both male and female sex parts)
• breed by releasing tough, egg-like structures

Entoprocts
(Endoprocts or Kamptozoans)
• about 150 species
• aquatic (live in water)
• mostly marine or sea-dwelling
• grow as rooted, branching colonies
• each animal has a C-shaped ring of tentacles for feeding
• breed by releasing tiny, young forms or larvae

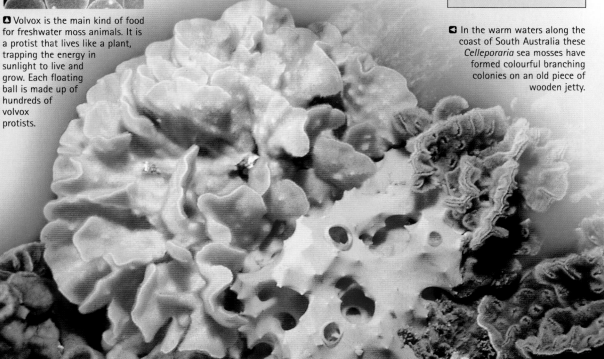

◪ Volvox is the main kind of food for freshwater moss animals. It is a protist that lives like a plant, trapping the energy in sunlight to live and grow. Each floating ball is made up of hundreds of volvox protists.

◪ In the warm waters along the coast of South Australia these *Celleporaria* sea mosses have formed colourful branching colonies on an old piece of wooden jetty.

15

SPONGES

SPONGES LOOK MORE LIKE PLANTS THAN ANIMALS. They grow on underwater objects such as rocks or plant stems. They cannot move around, although a few types twitch slightly at the surface when touched. They have no eyes or ears, brain or nerves, heart or blood. But they do catch their own food, by filtering tiny particles from water. The water enters the sponge through thousands of tiny holes, or pores, and then leaves through one of the few big holes. Adult sponges are fixed to the spot, but when they breed, they produce young ones or larvae, which swim actively. Eventually a larva finds a suitable place to settle down and grow into the adult colony of cells we call a sponge.

◀ Tiny coral animals (polyps) grow around a sponge's oscule – the main exit hole for water. The tunnels are visible inside the sponge's main body cavity.

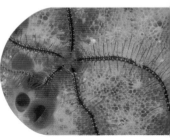

▲ A brittlestar climbs across an orange sponge.

◀ Breadcrumb sponges grow in several colours, including green (upper left). The hymenia sponge is usually blood-red (top right). Some solenia sponges are also red (top left). Column sponges can be purple or blue (centre). Vase sponges are wider, with one large exit hole for water (lower left). The brain sponge is pink (lower right).

◻ Different types of cup sponge grow in fresh and salt water.

A typical full-grown sponge is not so much one single animal, more a collection or colony of animal-like cells. These form a flask-shaped body surrounding a central cavity. There are many tiny holes or channels in the body wall, linking the cavity inside with the sea water outside. Whip-like flagella on cells lining the cavity beat to make a current of water flow through the channels into the central cavity. The water brings with it tiny bits of food such as protists, tiny seaweeds, and animal eggs and larvae. The water, and the sponge's waste products, pass out through larger channels, oscules, usually at the top.

◻ These pink sponges, on an old jetty support, form a network of chambers and holes used by worms, fish and other creatures.

BATH SPONGES

Most bath sponges are now made of plastic foam. But many years ago they were gathered from the sea. The common bath sponge lives on the sea bed, in clear, warm water. It is rather slimy, and is a yellow or purple colour. After it dies, its soft parts rot away to leave its flexible skeleton of fibres and spicules. This skeleton forms the sponge we use in the bath. Its thousands of tiny holes once let the living sponge suck in water. In some areas, such as parts of the Mediterranean Sea, so many bath sponges have been gathered that this animal is now very rare. It takes perhaps 20 years for a new bath sponge to grow.

HOW SPONGES BREED

Like many plants, sponges can reproduce by growing small extra parts, buds, which come away and grow into new sponges. Or they can breed sexually, like animals. Each sponge is both male and female, so it can make both sperm and eggs. An egg and sperm join, or fertilize, and develop into a tiny sponge larva which swims away. It lives in the open sea for a day or two, before settling on the sea bed to grow into a new adult sponge.

HOW DO SPONGES SURVIVE?

Sponges have no obvious defences. They cannot bite or sting. They cannot swim away. So how do they protect themselves? The bodies of many sponges are full of tiny, sharp spikes of hard minerals, such as lime, chalk or silica (the same substance that glass is made from). These spikes, called spicules, make up the sponge's skeleton. They give its body firmness. They also help to deter animals who might try to eat the sponge. In addition, many types of sponges have an unpleasant smell or a horrible taste, which also puts off their predators.

PLACOZOANS

These tiny animals, which grow to the size of an ant, resemble giant amoebas, but their bodies are made up of about 1,000 cells. Placozoans ooze and move like slugs. There are only a couple of species known and both live in the sea.

Sponges (Poriferans)	Placozoans
• about 10,000 species	• only a few species
• most live in the sea, a few in fresh water	• live in the sea
• many have spiky inner skeletons	• crawl along like slugs or giant amoebas
• body full of holes	• about 3 mm long
• some grow to 4 m across	

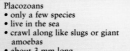

JELLYFISH

JELLYFISH RANGE IN SIZE FROM SMALLER THAN THE TIP OF YOUR FINGER TO GIANTS LARGER THAN A PATIO SUNSHADE UMBRELLA, MEASURING MORE THAN 1.8 m. But most are about the size and shape of a breakfast cereal bowl.

△ Haliclystus is a stalked jellyfish that lives in sheltered rock pools, clinging to seaweed.

Some types can swim weakly by making pulsing movements of the main body or bell – like opening and closing your fingers. But these swimming motions are weak and most jellyfish are at the mercy of strong ocean currents. They are often washed up helpless onto the shore after a storm. Their floppy bodies collapse, and these creatures soon dry out and die.

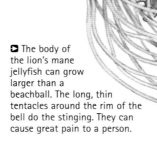

▶ The body of the lion's mane jellyfish can grow larger than a beachball. The long, thin tentacles around the rim of the bell do the stinging. They can cause great pain to a person.

▶ Stauromedusans, or stalked jellyfish, are jellyfish that think they are anemones. There is a stalk on the top of the bell with a sticky end that attaches to a piece of seaweed or sea grass.

SWIMMING JELLYFISH
Around the rim of the jellyfish's main body, or bell, is a ring of muscle fibres. These can be shortened or contracted to squeeze the bell like a purse-string and make pulsating movements, which propel water out of the bell and so push the jellyfish through the water. Usually a jellyfish swims upwards, to rise closer to the surface. When it stops swimming, it sinks down again. Using these movements the jellyfish can follow its prey, the small animals of the plankton, as they rise near the surface at night and sink to mid water during the day.

HOW JELLYFISH BREED
Jellyfish reproduce by releasing tiny young forms, or larvae. These swim off and settle on the sea bed, where they turn into small polyps. At this stage they resemble tiny see-through sea anemones, smaller than this o.

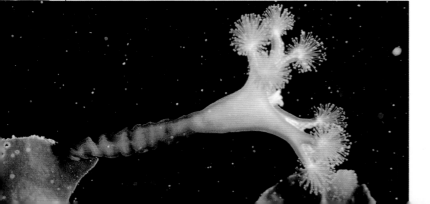

THE CNIDARIAN STING

A jellyfish has thousands of microscopic stinging cells, nematocysts, all along its tentacles. The cell "fires" a barbed dart that carries either a sticky, glue-like substance or a poison (venom). Each stinging cell has a lid covering the dart. Near the lid is a tiny trigger. When a prey animal touches the trigger, the lid springs open and the dart shoots out. Each stinging cell can only be used once, after which it breaks down, is absorbed into the jellyfish's body and replaced by a new stinging cell.

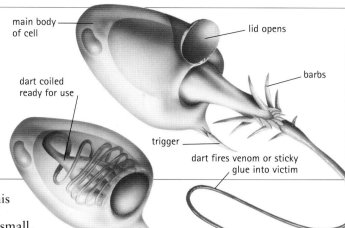

main body of cell

lid opens

barbs

dart coiled ready for use

trigger

dart fires venom or sticky glue into victim

Jellyfish polyps often spend winter in this form. In spring, each polyp form grows "buds". Each bud develops into a very small, star-shaped version of the adult animal. This is released and drifts away into the plankton.

BALANCING ACT

Jellyfish have no proper eyes. But they have special sense organs which can detect light or dark, and which also tell them which way is up or down. These pinhead-size sense organs are spaced around the edge of the bell. The animal uses them to tell the difference between day and night, and also to change its swimming direction according to the position of the sun.

PREDATORS

Even though jellyfish have poisonous stings, some animals eat them. Jellyfish predators include various kinds of fish, squid and especially sea turtles. However, because many jellyfish are pale or transparent this probably makes them harder for predators to see and catch.

FLOATING MOON

The moon jellyfish, aurelia, grows to about 40 cm across and has a bluish tinge. It is very numerous and can be seen in bays and estuaries close to shore, as well as in the open ocean far from land. Moon jellyfish feed on small members of the plankton, such as tiny shrimps and other crustaceans, and also on fish. These get stuck on the stinging cells, the lower surface of the bell, and the frilly oral arms, and are then transferred to the jellyfish's mouth. The moon jellyfish has a fringe of short stinging tentacles and four much longer feeding or oral tentacles. The pink horseshoe-shaped parts in the middle of its main body are its reproductive organs.

STALKED JELLYFISH

These unusual jellyfish live attached to rocks or seaweeds. They are small, growing only to the size of your little finger. They look like jellyfish that have turned upside down and become stuck by the top of the body, which is underneath. Stalked jellyfish can move to a different place by slowly cartwheeling along. They feed on tiny prey such as worms and copepods.

◘ The moon jellyfish (aurelia) is one of the most common jellyfish, found in seas throughout the world.

True jellyfish *(Scyphozoans)*
• about 200 species, all in the sea
• the main form or stage in the life cycle is the free-floating medusa
• the body is circular
• four-part symmetry, with four mouth or oral tentacles and four sets of reproductive organs
• sexes separate – a jellyfish is either female or male

ANEMONES AND PARTNERS

SEA ANEMONES ARE SIMPLE CREATURES. They have no proper brain, only a few nerves to control the movements of their tentacles and stalk. They can only do the simplest actions, such as detecting and eating prey, and gliding along the rocks to a new place. Yet anemones have many "friends" on the seashore. They live in

△ Shrimps are at home among anemones.

partnerships with other creatures such as fish, shrimps, crabs and worms. These other creatures have thick shells or coatings of body mucus (slime) that protect them from the anemone's stings. Usually, both partners benefit from being together. For example, the anemone feeds on leftovers from the food of its fish friend, while the fish is safe hiding in the anemone's tentacles. This type of helpful partnership in nature is called symbiosis.

Symbiosis happens between many types of creatures, such as cleaner fish and bigger fish, and oxpecker birds and cattle. But it is especially common among sea anemones. It has probably evolved gradually, over millions of years.

TOLERANT PARTNERS
As a result, the anemone has become used to the presence of another creature in its tentacles. It can detect this partner by the chemical substances that

△ This tiny porcelain crab is safe among the tentacles of an anemone. It scavenges small bits of food and keeps the anemone clean.

the partner gives off, and so rarely tries to sting it. At the same time, the partner has evolved some kind of protection against the anemone's stings, and is hardly ever hurt.

TYPES OF PARTNERS
Clown or anemone fish, usually striped orange and white, form symbiotic partnerships with anemones. So do various kinds of banded shrimps and crabs. Some hermit crabs allow calliactis sea anemones to live on the large sea snail shell that the crab uses as a mobile home. The anemone gets carried around and probably has more chance of finding prey. Meanwhile the crab is protected by the stinging partner attached to its shell.

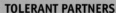

△ The sunstar above is not an anemone friend, but a victim. The large dahlia anemone is slowly pulling the sunstar, a type of starfish, into its mouth.

PLUMOSE ANEMONE

This type of sea anemone can stretch itself tall and thin, or pull down its stalk or column to be shorter and fatter. The anemone pictured here is halfway between these two positions. Plumose anemones occur in many colours, from almost perfect white through cream, yellow and brown to orange and red. They live in seashore pools, especially under rocky overhangs, and on and under breakwaters, piers and jetties. They can catch larger prey, but they mainly feed on tiny bits of floating food filtered from the water by the feathery tentacles.

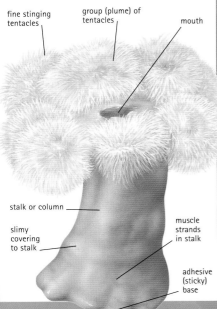

fine stinging tentacles

group (plume) of tentacles

mouth

stalk or column

slimy covering to stalk

muscle strands in stalk

adhesive (sticky) base

When one catches food, the other can share the leftover bits and pieces. The calliactis anemone is sometimes called the parasitic anemone. But it is not really a parasite, since it rarely does the hermit crab any harm. The two are usually equal partners, so a better name for it would be the symbiotic anemone.

MORE PARTNERSHIPS

Other crabs may grab anemones in their pincers, like underwater flaming torches. The crab waves the anemone, to scare away enemies or to try and sting possible prey. Again, both crab and anemone benefit from the relationship.

▶ Clownfish and their anemone partners are popular in tropical saltwater aquaria. The fish's thick coating of slime protects it against the anemone's stings.

CORALS

THERE ARE MORE THAN 5,000 DIFFERENT KINDS OF CORAL. A coral animal or polyp is usually less than 1 cm tall, and looks like a miniature sea anemone. In fact,

△ Red-tipped soft corals

corals are very close cousins of anemones. Most types of corals are found in tropical seas. Some coral polyps live singly, but most live with others of their kind, linked or connected into huge groups or colonies. Some build stony protective casings around themselves. This is how the rocks of a coral reef gradually build up. Sea fans are coral polyps that make tough, horny skeletons which branch into a tree or fan-like shape. The protective cases of soft corals are more like spongy, rubbery jelly.

△ Some soft corals form colourful, branching, finger-like structures that are tough and leathery.

▽ The reef rocks made by coral polyps have many holes, crevices, caves and overhangs. These are ideal places for larger animals to hide.

Coral animals are cnidarians. They catch their prey with sticky or stinging tentacles, like sea anemones and jellyfish. But, unlike jellyfish, corals do not have a medusa or floating stage in their lives. Like anemones, all coral animals are polyps. In a coral colony, each polyp is connected to its neighbour by living tissue, usually at its base. So the whole colony is joined, almost like one giant multi-animal.

Each polyp can catch its own tiny victims, but the food may then be shared among the nearby members of the colony. This is important because in some corals, certain polyps cannot feed for themselves. Instead, they help to protect or support the colony, by building cases or outer skeletons.

HIDING FROM ENEMIES

In stony corals, each polyp makes a cup-shaped skeleton beneath itself, from rock minerals that it takes out of the sea water. When danger threatens, such as a polyp-eating fish or starfish, the polyp retreats into this protective cup. It emerges again later when the danger is past.

HOW CORALS EAT

A feeding polyp spreads its little tentacles in the sea water. It relies on currents and waves to bring fresh supplies of food, usually with each tide. It catches tiny protists and animals as they drift past. These stick to the tentacles and are then passed to the mouth at the centre, just as in the larger anemones. Many coral polyps come out to feed only at night. This is when sea plankton rise nearer the surface. The polyps wave their shiny tentacles and make a patch of coral rock look like a glistening, multicoloured, living carpet.

BREEDING

When conditions are right, usually on a calm night when the moon is full, all the corals in one area release their eggs and sperm into the sea. These float near the surface in great clouds.

◀ This bright, night-time coral reef scene shows various kinds of coral, anemones, sponges and fish such as seahorses and wrasses. By day, most coral polyps withdraw into their protective cases.

◢ At breeding time, coral animals release clouds of eggs and sperm that drift away in the seawater.

Each sperm joins with, or fertilizes, an egg. The fertilized egg develops into a tiny coral larva that floats in the sea for a short time. Then it swims down to the sea bed to find a resting place. The larva sticks itself firmly onto a rock, and grows into a tiny coral polyp, complete with a ring of tentacles. After several weeks, if the single original polyp survives, it has sprouted or budded several new polyps. These remain joined together. As their numbers increase and spread, they gradually form a new coral colony.

INSIDE A CORAL POLYP

A coral animal is like a miniature sea anemone. Its stalk is almost all stomach or digestive cavity. Folds of flesh called mesenteries stick into the cavity, forming a larger surface area for absorbing digested nutrients.

tentacles

mouth

pharynx

stomach (gastro-ventricular cavity or enteron)

tentacles contain branches of main cavity

mesentery folds

body or stalk

stomach filaments (acontia) can be stuck out through mouth if danger threatens

fleshy folds at base of stalk

hard, stony base

TYPES OF CORAL

• stony or hard corals, usually colonial – some are reef-builders
• soft corals
• gorgonian corals, also called sea fans and sea whips (types of soft coral)

23

▶ The octopus trails
its tentacles behind
it as it jets through
the water.

SECTION 2
WORMS, SNAILS & STARFISH

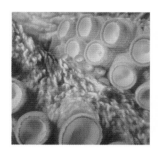   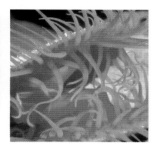

MANY LONG, THIN, SOFT, SLIMY, WRIGGLY CREATURES ARE CALLED WORMS. They are not very appealing to most people. Yet worms are some of the most varied and important members of the animal kingdom. There are at least 20 major groups of worm, ranging from common earthworms that keep the soil fertile, to tiny parasitic worms that cause horrible diseases, to giant tubeworms as thick as your arm living in pitch blackness at the bottom of the sea.

The mollusc group is not well known to many people. Yet it is second only to insects, in the number of different species. Most molluscs have a hard protective shell around the soft body. The group includes limpets and whelks on the seashore, snails in gardens and water snails in ponds. Some molluscs are eaten as food, such as oysters, mussels, scallops and clams. A few, like cone shells, are deadly poisonous. And one of the largest of all animals, the giant squid of the ocean depths, is a mollusc.

Yet another enormous group of sea-dwelling animals is the echinoderms, meaning "spiny-skinned". Starfish, urchins, brittlestars, featherstars and sea lilies are all echinoderms. One of the strangest is the sea cucumber. It looks like an animated sausage eating slimy ooze on the sea bed. If it is attacked, it sicks up sticky threads from its stomach and squirts them out of its mouth!

EARTHWORMS AND LEECHES

THERE ARE AT LEAST 30 DIFFERENT GROUPS OF WORM-LIKE CREATURES. The main group is the annelids or segmented worms, also called true worms. An annelid worm has a body divided into lots of similar ring-like sections called segments. There are 12,000 species of annelid worms, including familiar earthworms, lugworms and ragworms on the seashore, and leeches. Although these animals are amazingly numerous, we rarely see them because most worms live only in water or under the ground in damp mud, sand or soil. This is because worms absorb oxygen through their thin, moist skin. If the skin dries out, the worm dies. Worms are also soft, slow-moving and vulnerable, so they gain some protection from living in tubes and tunnels.

▶ The horse leech grows to 30 cm long. It swallows tiny animals whole.

◀ Most of these tropical fanworms (page 28) are hidden in purple-tinged tubes. Two have spread their spiral yellow feeding tentacles.

DELICIOUS WORMS

Worms have few defences against predators, except their underground lifestyle and ability to breed in great numbers. Birds such as thrushes and blackbirds depend on plentiful supplies of worms for themselves and their chicks. Some birds even trample on the soil to mimic the patter of raindrops, which brings the worms to the surface.

▶ A spiral fanworm's feathery tentacles are covered with sticky mucus, which traps tiny bits of food and flows slowly into its mouth.

Earthworms spend nearly all their lives underground, burrowing in the soil. They push aside some earth and swallow the rest. The earth passes through the worm's gut and nutritious bits like pieces of dead leaves are digested. The remains pass out of the worm's rear end as fine-grained droppings. These are left as curly worm casts at the surface. Millions of earthworms keep soil fertile. They break down and recycle plant and animal remains. Their burrows allow air and moisture into the soil, for plant roots to use, and to help water drain away.

◳ Two earthworms partly emerge from their tunnels on a damp night, to mate. They lie side by side and exchange sperm.

MATING IN THE GRASS

An earthworm has no obvious head. The front or mouth end is slightly more pointed than the rear end, and it has simple detectors that can distinguish between light and dark, but which cannot form an image like proper eyes. One obvious feature of the earthworm is a part called the saddle or clitellum, where several segments seem to be enlarged and fused together. When two worms meet to mate, they put their saddles next to each other. Each earthworm is an hermaphrodite – it has both male and female parts. So each passes sperm to the other, to fertilize its eggs. Each then forms a cocoon of eggs around the saddle. The cocoon slips off and is left in the soil, and baby worms hatch from it.

◳ A leech moves by "looping". It stretches forwards while anchored by its back sucker, and sticks down the front one. Then it detaches the rear sucker, shortens its body, attaches the rear sucker again, and so on.

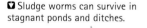

◲ Sludge worms can survive in stagnant ponds and ditches.

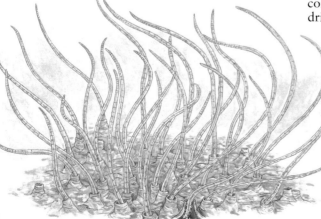

WATER WORMS

The bright red tubifex or sludge worm is a cousin of the earthworm. It lives in fresh water, and is sometimes called the bloodworm because of its colour. The bright red is due to a pigment (coloured substance) that is specialized to take in oxygen from the water, through the skin into the worm's body. The pigment is so plentiful that this worm can live in stagnant water that is very low in oxygen. Hundreds of sludge worms build tubes of sticky mucus in the mud and wave their tails in the water to obtain oxygen.

THE BLOOD-SUCKERS

Leeches are like flattened types of worms. They have muscular bodies which can shorten or lengthen, and a sucker at each end. Some leeches prey on smaller worms, insect grubs and similar creatures. Others are parasites, sucking the blood of fish or other animals, including people. The hungry leech clamps itself onto an animal as it passes, perhaps while coming to water to drink. It then rubs its way into the skin with three sets of tiny teeth and gorges itself, sucking in five times its own weight of blood and fluids. The leech can survive for weeks before needing another meal.

BIGGEST... !
The world's largest earthworms are giant Gippsland earthworms of Australia. Most are over 90 cm long. But the biggest grow to more than 6.5 m long.

ANNELID WORMS
- about 12,000 species
- tube-shaped soft body
- divided into segments

Three main subgroups:
Earthworms
- 3,000 species
- most live in soil or fresh water
- hermaphrodite (each individual is both male and female)
- includes most earthworms, also sludge worms (bloodworms)

Leeches
- 500 species
- many are leaf-shaped
- mostly freshwater, some in the sea or on land
- some are blood-suckers
- hermaphrodite

Bristleworms
Described on page 28

27

BRISTLEWORMS

BRISTLEWORMS ARE NAMED FROM THE STIFF BRISTLE-LIKE HAIRS, KNOWN AS CHAETAE, STICKING OUT ALL OVER THEIR BODIES. More than half of the types of segmented worms (page 26) belong to the

🔺 Feeding fanworms

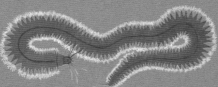

🔺 Ragworm

bristleworm group, also called polychaetes. In some types the bristles are attached to paddle-like flaps. Bristleworms live mainly in the sea, and use these flaps as oars, to paddle over the bottom or dig into sand and mud. Some kinds live inside tubes.

Compared to earthworms, most bristleworms have an obvious head and tail end. The head usually has tentacles, which may look like thin fingers, or be arranged as a frilly ring or a feathery crown. Some types of bristleworms also have simple types of eyes that can pick out shapes. There may be a pair of long thread-like feelers at the tail end.

Bristleworms on the shore include ragworms and lugworms. Ragworms often live in burrows lined with their own hardened mucus (slime), in the muddy silt that collects at the bottom of a rock pool. When the tide is out, the ragworm stays hidden. When the tide comes in, the ragworm emerges from its burrow to feed on the surface of the mud. It can wriggle like a snake, or swim by rowing with its paddle-like flaps.

Ragworms eat a range of food, from dead animals and small creatures such as shrimps to seaweeds. Their strong jaws can easily bite chunks of flesh from a carcass – and even draw blood through human skin. They can also shed their slimy body covering and eat it, to take in the microbes in the slime.

FAN-FEEDERS

The main body of a fanworm stays hidden inside a protective tube set into the sea bed, which it builds from mud or sand particles glued together with its own slimy mucus. Fanworms are named for their stiff, feathery feeding tentacles, which they stick out from the top of the tube and spread out like a fan. One of the most beautiful fanworms is the peacock worm. Its tube may be 25 cm long. When safe, it extends the tentacles and waves them in the water. The tentacles are coated with a thin layer of sticky mucus that catches any bits of food floating past. They also work as gills for breathing.

If a fish or other predator swims nearby, the peacock worm whisks in its tentacles and pulls itself down into the safety of its tube. Sometimes peacock worms and other fanworms live in groups, looking like a carpet of flowers. When danger appears, they are gone in a flash, leaving the sea bed looking bare and lifeless.

28

▶ Lugworms hide under the sand in U-shaped burrows. The worm wriggles to make water flow through its burrow, so it can breathe.

WHITE TUBEWORMS

At the bottom of the sea, giant white tubeworms live near vents that pour out scalding, sulphur-rich water. They are 3 m long and as thick as your arm. They take in the sulphur chemicals, and bacteria in their bodies use the chemicals to make food, which they share with the worm.

HARD TUBES

Some bristleworms build much tougher, more rigid tubes from chalky minerals, either in the sand or on rocks. The hard, white, wiggly tubes on seashore weeds and boulders belong to bristleworms called keelworms. When the tide is in, the keelworm pushes its tiny crown of feeding tentacles from the end of the tube, to gather food.

SAND CASTS

Little mounds of sand or mud on the shore are the casts of lugworms. These worms are 15–20 cm long, soft, and thicker at the front end. They feed like earthworms, by eating the sand or mud, digesting any nutrients, and then passing out the remains as the familiar worm cast.

THE MOUSE WORM

The sea mouse is not a mouse at all, but a type of bristleworm. It grows about 20 cm long. Its plump, humped body is covered with grey-brown, hairy flaps, almost like the fur of a real mouse. Sea mice live mainly on muddy or sandy sea beds, in the Atlantic Ocean and Mediterranean Sea.

☑ The tubes of peacock worms partly stick up from the sea bed.

(continued from page 27)

Bristleworms
• 8,500 species
• most live in the sea
• body has bristles or flaps
• sexes separate (male or female)
• includes lugworms, ragworms, fanworms, peacock worms, sea mice, scaleworms, catworms

THE RANGE OF MOLLUSCS

SNAILS AND SLUGS, AND SEA CREATURES SUCH AS WHELKS, COCKLES, CLAMS AND MUSSELS, ARE ALL MOLLUSCS. So are octopuses, squid and cuttlefish. Indeed, there are nearly 100,000 species of mollusc, making up the second largest group of animals after insects and other arthropods. They vary greatly in size and shape, but all have soft bodies, and many have hard shells. Most molluscs move about on a large, flat pad, called the foot. The head of a mollusc often has soft, bendy tentacles, used for feeling its way about or grasping food.

The bright colours and patterns of tropical sea slugs warn that they are bad to eat. The knobs and frills help in breathing.

Sea slugs look like multicoloured snails without their shells. They crawl around on the sea bed looking for food.

The octopus trails its tentacles behind it as it jets through the water.

edges of the mantle ooze a mineral-rich, liquid substance. This hardens, and the shell grows with its owner.

The shells of some molluscs are round and smooth. Some are coiled into tight spirals, or spread out like fans. A bivalve's shell is two flap-like shell halves, called valves, hinged together. In molluscs such as slugs and cuttlefish, the shell is inside the body. If there is no shell, the mantle forms a leathery cover around the body.

Most molluscs live in the sea. Only certain species of two groups, the bivalves and the snails, live in fresh water. Some snails are even able to live in damp conditions on land. There are seven main groups of molluscs. The three most familiar are the gastropods such as snails, limpets and winkles; the bivalves such as mussels, clams, oysters and razorshells; and the cephalopods such as octopuses, cuttlefish, nautiluses and squid.

All molluscs have a large, cloak-like part around the main body, called the mantle. In many molluscs, this makes a hard, protective shell on the outside, which the creature can withdraw into, to avoid danger. The shell grows as the

Many molluscs look like little more than squishy blobs. But the body is quite complicated inside, containing many of the usual important parts such as a brain, heart and kidney. Muscles can pull and squeeze the body into almost any shape.

Scallops are bivalve molluscs, which means they have two shell parts. The scallop can snap its shell shut to swim jerkily.

◪ Tusk shells
have long, curving,
tapering shells that
look like elephants' tusks.
The shell is open at both
ends. The tusk shell lives half buried, head-down in the sand.
It feeds by spreading its thread-like tentacles into the sand.

THE MOLLUSC'S FOOT

The mollusc's large, muscular, pad-like foot is
used for many tasks. Squid and octopuses have
developed the foot into tentacles to catch prey. A
limpet uses its sucker foot to cling to rocks. A
snail slides about on its foot. A clam's foot is like
a strong finger that pokes and digs into the sand
or mud. A razorshell's foot is so powerful, it can
dig the animal down into the seashore mud,
almost as fast as a person could dig with a spade.

◪ Chitons are oval in shape
and have a shell divided into
eight arched plates, making
them look as if they are
protected by chain-mail
armour. The alternative name
for this group is "coat-of-mail
shells". They graze on the film
of seaweed covering rocks in
shallow water along the coast.
Chitons can curl up tightly if
dislodged from their rocks.

THE MOLLUSC'S RADULA

One special feature of molluscs is a file-like
"tongue" called a radula, covered in rows
of hard teeth. The mollusc uses this to
scrape away at its food, perhaps tiny
seaweeds covering a rock, or lettuces in
the garden. Not all molluscs feed in this
way, however. Squid and octopuses are
active predators, tearing up prey with a
beak-like mouth.

FOOD FROM MOLLUSCS

All over the
world, people
like to eat
molluscs –
favourites
include
oysters, clams,
cockles, mussels,
scallops, abalones,
winkles, octopus and
squid. They are
usually an important
source of food in
coastal places and
on islands. Some
molluscs have become
rare or endangered as
a result of being over-
collected for food.

◪ Many mollusc shells are
incredibly beautiful, especially
when wet from the sea. The
tropical conch shell is especially
attractive. Empty, it has been used
as a trumpet to make sounds for
thousands of years. However, the
souvenir trade in mollusc shells
endangers many species.

◪ Mussels are fixed to
seashore rocks by strong,
stringy byssus threads.

MOLLUSCS

- up to 100,000 species
- most live in the sea, some in fresh water, a few on land
- soft body in cloak-like mantle
- many have hard shell around body
- many have large, muscular base or foot
- some have flexible tentacles

Main groups of molluscs:
Tusk shells
- 350 species
- marine
- burrow into sand
- single shell shaped like elephant's tusk

Slugs and snails
- 70,000 species
- marine, freshwater and land-living
- most have a single shell, often coiled

- head has tentacles
- glide on muscular foot

Bivalves
- 20,000 species
- most are marine, some freshwater
- hinged shell of two parts (valves)
- foot rounded, not flattened
- most burrow, or live attached to rocks

Squid and octopuses
- 650 species
- live in the sea
- long tentacles around mouth
- large eyes, big brains
- hide in rocks or swim in the sea

Chitons
- 550 species
- live in the sea, on rocks on the shore, or in shallow water
- body oval and domed (like a woodlouse), with eight plates
- no eyes

SLUGS AND SNAILS

LAND SNAILS AND SEA SNAILS, LAND SLUGS AND SEA SLUGS, ALONG WITH LIMPETS AND WHELKS, ARE ALL GASTROPODS – MOLLUSCS WITH SOFT, SQUIDGY BODIES. The name gastropod means "stomach-foot", because these molluscs seem to slide along on their stomachs. But it is really the same muscular foot possessed by all molluscs. Many snails and limpets have a hard shell, so gastropods are sometimes called univalves (meaning "one shell"). A slug's soft body is exposed.

◙ Some sea slugs have large hair-like tentacles on their backs. These can carry stings or horrible-tasting fluids.

◁ Few molluscs are more familiar than the common garden snail. After a heavy rainstorm, snails emerge as if from nowhere in the damp conditions. They rasp their way through many kinds of leaves and plant bits on the ground.

When a gastropod slides along the ground, its large, flat stomach-foot spreads out underneath. Muscles in the foot ripple backwards and forwards. Land snails and slugs ooze a trail of slime to ease the way forward and reduce friction.

THE SHELL'S TRAPDOOR
On the back of the foot, most sea snails and some land snails have a flap called an operculum. When danger threatens, the snail retreats into its shell and pulls the operculum over the opening, like closing a trapdoor, for protection.

Many gastropods have four tentacles on the head. Two are feelers that help them to find their way by touch.

The other two are often stalks with eyes at the tip. But many gastropods have no eyes at all.

SHELLS AND SURVIVAL
Snails seem to live everywhere, not only in all parts of the oceans, but in almost all habitats on land. Like all molluscs, the snail needs plenty of moisture to survive. So land snails stay in or near moist places. If the weather is too cold or too dry, the snail makes a seal of slime over its shell entrance. This hardens into a kind of temporary door. In the autumn, in temperate regions, many snails settle down for the winter in this state. As it gets warmer in the spring, the snail breaks open the seal and emerges again. In hot, dry weather, snails also seal themselves in their shells and wait for cooler, moister conditions. Surviving heat or dryness like this is called aestivation.

MALE AND FEMALE
Snails are hermaphrodite, which means that each animal is both male and female at the same time. When they mate, each snail passes sperm into the body of the other snail. Each partner goes on to develop and lay a clutch of leathery eggs. There may be dozens of eggs in a single clutch.

LARGEST... !
The biggest snail is the African giant snail. Its huge shell can be almost 25 cm across.

JELLY BABIES !
Water and pond snails lay their eggs in a string or blob of jelly, usually stuck to the stem of a water plant or stone. The jelly helps to protect the eggs from being eaten, and also stops them drying out if the water level in the pond or stream changes. In an aquarium tank water snails often lay their eggs on the glass. This allows a clear view of the tiny baby snails developing inside.

◙ Slugs like this keeled slug have a great appetite for all kinds of plants, including potatoes. The keeled slug often burrows under the soil, especially to eat plant roots and to hide during the day.

Eventually many tiny snails hatch. Except for their size, they look very like the adults, each with its tiny shell. It takes about two years for a snail to reach maturity.

SLUGS

Slugs are like snails that have lost their protective shells, although some slugs do have small shells inside their bodies, just under the skin of the back. Some even have a tiny shell on the back. To protect themselves, slugs produce large quantities of very sticky slime, which puts off many predators. The slime also helps to stop the slugs from drying out. However, some birds, such as thrushes, and some mammals, including hedgehogs, can cope with this slime. They eat large numbers of slugs. Song thrushes can even tackle snails. They bash the snail against a hard object, like a stone, until its shell breaks open. Then they quickly eat the tasty flesh inside.

⬧ This Indonesian sea slug can swim by undulating its cape-like foot. The gills are tall, yellow and spiky. Sea slugs eat seaweeds and small animals such as sea mats and corals that coat rocks.

⬧ Most snails are little bigger than cherries. But a few, such as the giant ram's-horn snail of ponds and lakes, can be 10 to 15 cm across.

SLUGS AT SEA

The marine relatives of snails and slugs include some of the most beautiful of all sea creatures. Like land slugs, sea slugs are mostly without shells. Many of them have feathery gills and bodies covered with amazingly bright, almost glowing patterns and colours. There are sea slugs in shades of orange, pink or blue, and with tufts of vividly brilliant gills on their backs. The bright colours warn predators that they should be left alone. Sea slugs taste horrible, and some even have poisonous stings on their backs.

⬧ Sea slugs are also called nudibranchs. This yellow-spotted red nudibranch is from the seas around the Philippines.

GROUPS OF SLUGS
(continued from page 31):

Land and freshwater snails, slugs
• 20,500 species
• on land and in fresh water
• spiral or coiled shell (not in slugs)

Sea slugs
• 1,250 species
• mostly slug-like, lacking shells
• bright colours
• frilly gills

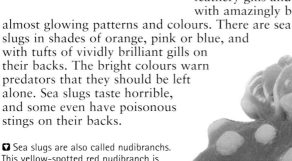

SQUID, OCTOPUSES AND CUTTLEFISH

◩ The pearly nautilus floats slowly in mid water with its tentacles pulled in (above).

◩ Octopus tentacles are covered in suckers, which they use to hold their prey and to move over the rocks.

THE MOST FASCINATING OF ALL MOLLUSCS ARE SQUID AND OCTOPUSES. They are called cephalopods, a name that means "head-footed", because their molluscan foot is at the head end and has lots of long tentacles. They have the typical mollusc's soft body, but only the squid has a shell, which is small and rod-shaped, and inside the body. These creatures are fierce predators. Squid swim very fast, and octopuses hide away in caves and holes in the rocks. Squid and octopuses can squirt out an ink-like liquid if they are attacked. This makes the water cloudy, allowing the mollusc to escape to safety.

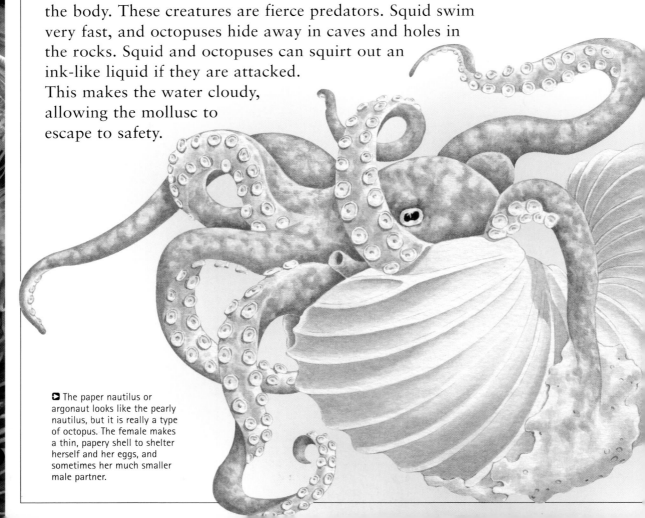

◪ The paper nautilus or argonaut looks like the pearly nautilus, but it is really a type of octopus. The female makes a thin, papery shell to shelter herself and her eggs, and sometimes her much smaller male partner.

Squid are narrow and streamlined, with flap-like fins at one end to keep them steady in the water. They have large eyes and good vision, to track their prey in the ocean. To catch food, they use a long pair of tentacles, which have adhesive suckers at the end. They have eight shorter tentacles too, also with suckers. Squid move slowly by rippling their fins, or dart suddenly using a kind of jet-propulsion, squirting water rapidly out of the siphon (breathing tube).

Some kinds of squid can produce lights inside their bodies. They have special body parts to create the light, and some can even direct the light like a torch. This is very useful in the dark depths of the sea.

CUTTLEFISH

Cuttlefish are like small, flattened squid, with a fin running around all sides of the body. Even more than squid, they are the chameleons of the sea, able to change colour and pattern in a split second.

A cuttlefish holds its tentacles together for streamlining as it swims.

The skin of a cuttlefish is patterned with tiny spots of different colours – yellow, red, brown and black. The animal can control the size of these by muscles, and make many different shades by mixing the amounts of each colour.

LARGEST... !

The giant squid of the ocean depths is the largest mollusc, and also the largest animal without a backbone. It reaches a maximum length of about 17 m from the tip of its outstretched tentacles to its tail end. Its eyes are the largest in the animal kingdom, at more than 40 cm across. The smallest squid are only about 1 cm long.

The blue-ringed octopus of the Indian and Pacific region is only small, but has a very poisonous bite. The rings on its body glow bright blue if it is threatened.

OCTOPUSES

An octopus has a sack-like body, large eyes, and eight long tentacles used for catching prey. Like other cephalopods, its beak-like mouth is hidden in the middle of the ring of tentacles, where they join the body. Octopuses have complicated behaviour and are often said to be the most intelligent invertebrates. They can recognize different shapes, choosing the correct one to obtain food. They can also remember simple tasks, such as how to open a food box.

The common octopus of the Atlantic varies in size, but can reach about 90 cm in body length, with a tentacle spread of 3 m. Octopuses are rarely seen. They spend most of the day holed up in crevices in the rocks. They come out mainly at night, to hunt for other molluscs, crabs and similar prey. They also scavenge for dead meat.

THE NAUTILUS

Only one kind of cephalopod has a proper external shell like other molluscs. This is the nautilus, which has a shiny shell curled over its body. It swims along the sea bed, using its 35 or so tentacles to find prey. Unlike its cousins, it cannot squirt ink to hide and escape danger.

CEPHALOPOD MOLLUSCS

Octopuses, squid and cuttlefish
• 650 species
• marine
• streamlined shape (squid and cuttlefish)
• ten tentacles in squid and cuttlefish, eight in octopus

Nautiluses
• 6 species
• marine
• large spiral shell
• many tentacles

STARFISH AND SEASTARS

⬥ Sun star

STARFISH AND THEIR RELATIVES ARE CALLED ECHINODERMS. This means "hedgehog skin", and many of them are indeed very spiny. These creatures are numerous and widespread, but they all live in the sea, so many are unfamiliar. They have a body built around a radial plan, like the spokes of a wheel, rather than the bilateral or two-sided bodies of other animals. They also have tiny, flexible tube feet that end in suckers, for walking and feeding. As well as starfish, this group includes feather stars, sea lilies, sea urchins and sea cucumbers.

⬥ Sea lily (crinoid)

Most groups of sea animals have a few species adapted to life in fresh water or even dry land. Echinoderms do not. These creatures are quite large, and many are brightly coloured and easy to see, especially as they are slow-moving.

MANY ARMS

Many species of starfish have five arms, but some have seven, and others as many as 14. The upper side of the body usually has small, hard plates or spines embedded in the skin, for protection. Underneath, each arm has rows of tiny tube feet, like miniature sucker-ended fingers. The arms bend so that the starfish can glide across the sea bed.

▾ Starfish are flat, and have arms that spread out from the centre in a star-like pattern.

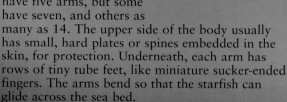

ARMED! ⚠

If a starfish is damaged and loses part of an arm, it can re-grow the missing piece again. The new part is often slightly smaller. Sometimes it branches into two, giving a six-armed starfish!

POISONOUS CORAL-EATER

The crown-of-thorns starfish eats small coral animals called polyps. Sometimes these starfish gather in such large numbers that they eat away an entire coral reef. They are covered with sharp, poisonous spines as defence.

Starfish are very strong and can prise open the shells of clams and other bivalve molluscs. When attacking its victim, the starfish arches over it and clamps a couple of arms onto each side. It then pulls with great strength and stamina. As the two parts of the mollusc's shell begin to gape, the starfish turns its stomach inside out, through its mouth and into the gap in the shell. It then begins to digest the prey's flesh. Eventually, the shell opens wide and the starfish completes its meal.

SOME TYPES OF STARFISH

Common starfish are indeed common. They sometimes gather in huge numbers over about 2.5 square kilometres of sea bed, moving slowly as they feed on bivalves and other molluscs, worms, crabs and also other echinoderms. These vast marauding columns of starfish leave a trail of dead and dying sea bed animals in their wake.

➤ Starfish look harmless, but they are all predators.

The sand star lives on fine sand, where it often lurks, half buried. It has a beautiful star shape, and its five arms are edged with spines. The common sun star is bright red, with as many as 14 short arms, spreading out sun-like from its large central disc. Its prey includes the common starfish.

WRITHING ARMS

The brittlestar (shown on page 16) is indeed brittle. Parts of its long, delicate arms often break off. The five arms spread out from a small central disc, and can loop back on themselves as the creature writhes speedily across the sea bed.

Most brittlestars live below the tide zone, in deeper water. They can sometimes be found piled up in huge heaps, with 1,000 individuals on just a few square metres of the sea bed. Most brittlestars feed by gathering up small edible items from the mud, or by filtering them from the water. The common brittlestar of the Atlantic and Mediterranean regions is a filter-feeder. It lives in dense colonies, with each animal waving its spiny arms to catch anything edible that may float past.

FEATHERY ARMS

Feather stars are similar to starfish and have feathery arms, used for both feeding and swimming. Many have ten arms, but some species may have almost 200! Feather stars grasp onto rocks or seaweeds and can also creep about. They feed by waving their arms in the water to filter out edible particles.

LILIES IN THE SEA

Sea lilies are close relatives of feather stars and feed in a similar way. Each animal is attached by a stalk to the sea bed, usually deep in the ocean. The stalk may be more than 90 cm long. They look like flowers on stalks, hence their name.

➤ This starfish is humped over its prey, dissolving and absorbing its flesh.

ECHINODERMS	Brittlestars
• 6,250 species	• 2,000 species
• live in the sea	• flat and star-shaped
• five-rayed (spoked) body plan	• usually five arms (sometimes six,
• inner skeleton, often spiny	or branched)
• tiny tube-like feet	• arms long and brittle
Three of the main groups:	Feather stars and sea lilies
	• 625 species (mostly feather stars)
Starfish	• either swimming (feather stars) or
• 1,500 species	stalked (sea lilies)
• flat and star-shaped	• feed by filtering seawater
• usually five arms (sometimes more)	

◭ Most moths fly at night.

SECTION 3
INSECTS & OTHER ARTHROPODS

THERE ARE AT LEAST 5 MILLION DIFFERENT KINDS, OR SPECIES, OF ANIMALS. And at least 80 out of every 100 species are insects. They range from tiny gnats and fairy flies, almost too small to see, to fist-sized beetles, and moths with wings as long as your hands. Three key features of insects help to make them so successful, widespread and diverse. These are: a hard outer body casing (exoskeleton), wings for flying and six legs with flexible joints for fast running.

Other animals have a tough outer body casing and jointed limbs, too. They include eight-legged spiders and scorpions (arachnids), and multi-legged centipedes and millipedes. Most insects do not live in the sea. But another huge group of joint-limbed creatures does – crustaceans such as crabs, lobsters, prawns, shrimps and krill. Most people are not familiar with creatures of the open ocean. So they rarely see one of the world's most numerous kinds of animal – the small flea-like crustaceans known as copepods.

All of the above creatures belong to the animal group known as arthropods. This name means "jointed legs". The arthropod's body casing and limb design have allowed this group to conquer all the Earth's habitats – from high mountains, hot springs and salty lakes, to dark caves and the deepest seas.

THE WORLD OF BUGS

THERE ARE PROBABLY MORE THAN TEN MILLION DIFFERENT KINDS, OR SPECIES, OF ANIMALS. Of these, possibly nine out of ten are bugs and other insects. The insects belong to a larger animal group known as the arthropods, which means "joint-limbed". The leg has rigid sections linked by flexible joints – similar to our own arms and legs. Insects and other arthropods also share another main feature – a hard outer covering to the body, called the cuticle. It forms a protective casing known as an exoskeleton, which covers the arthropod's body like a suit of armour. Ants, beetles, bugs, cockroaches, flies, fleas, bees and other insects, which all have six legs, are arthropods. So are the eight-legged arachnids such as spiders and scorpions, the multi-legged centipedes and millipedes, and crustaceans such as crabs, lobsters and shrimps. For every human being alive today, there are probably at least one million insects and other arthropods.

◯ Social insects live in groups, often in huge nests like this termite mound. Other social insects are ants, bees and wasps.

◯ Dragonflies are among the biggest flying insects.

Arthropods are mostly small. But they affect people the world over. Some are harmful. Termites eat away wooden buildings and bridges. Locusts devastate vast areas of crops. Wasps annoy us with their stings, and lice with their blood-sucking bites. Poisonous spiders and scorpions can cause great pain, even death. Serious diseases are spread by some arthropods, such as malaria by mosquitoes, plague by fleas and Lyme's disease by ticks.

INSIDE AN INSECT

An insect's body is divided into three main sections – head, thorax (chest) and abdomen. Most insects have three pairs of legs and one or two pairs of wings, all attached to the thorax. (The worker ant, as shown here, lacks wings.)

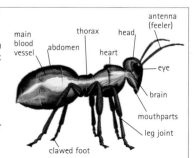

main blood vessel · abdomen · thorax · head · antenna (feeler) · heart · eye · brain · mouthparts · leg joint · clawed foot

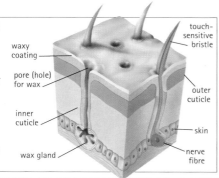

Mites are tiny arthropods related to spiders. Some live in soil. Others are parasites and suck blood from animals.

USEFUL ARTHROPODS

Some arthropods are useful to both people and plants. Bees make honey and carry pollen for flowers. Predatory insects such as lacewings eat plant pests such as aphids (which are also arthropods). Silkworms are really moth caterpillars that spin silk. Dung beetles help to recycle animal droppings. Small flies called fruit flies, drosophila, have been used as insect "guinea pigs" to unlock the secrets of how genes work.

SENSES

Most arthropods have keen senses, especially sight, smell and touch. Each eye is made of a cluster of separate units, each with its own lens. This design is called a compound eye. Arthropods cannot see as much detail as we can, but most are excellent at detecting small movements, and many insects can see different colours.

Arthropods use their feelers or antennae to smell and even "taste" the air or water around them, detecting tiny particles of scents and odours. The antennae and the tiny hair-like bristles on the body and legs can also detect the slightest touch and movements such as wind or water currents.

Grasshoppers and crickets have powerful chewing "jaws". In most insects these move from side to side rather than up and down.

WHERE INSECTS LIVE

Insects are found in almost every corner of the Earth, on land and in the air – in forests and grasslands, deserts, marshes and wetlands, streams and lakes, even high on mountains and glaciers, and deep in pitch-dark caves. Our parks and gardens, and even our houses, also buzz and crawl with insects. They include houseflies and ants, fleas on pets, and silverfish in dark cupboards. Insects have not colonized the sea itself, although they live on coastal land.

OTHER ARTHROPOD HABITATS

Spiders, scorpions, centipedes and millipedes thrive mainly in warmer countries, especially among the dead leaves of the tropical forest floor and high above among the tree leaves. Most crustaceans, from tiny copepods to huge crabs and lobsters, live in the sea. Some, like crayfish and water fleas, dwell in fresh water. A few, like woodlice, can survive in damp places on land.

AN ARTHROPOD'S COVERING

The arthropod's body is covered by the cuticle, which is thin and light, yet strong and tough. It is made mainly from a substance called chitin. In land arthropods such as insects, the cuticle has a waxy, waterproof covering. In order to grow, an arthropod must shed its cuticle, and grow a new, bigger one underneath. This process is known as moulting or ecdysis.

Insects
- more than one million species
- body divided into three main parts
- three pairs of legs
- most have two pairs of wings
- live on land and in fresh water

Crustaceans
- 43,000 species
- body divided into three main parts
- many have a hard, shell-like casing
- several pairs of legs
- two pairs of feelers
- most live in the sea

King Crabs
- 5 species
- heavy, rounded outer shell
- long tail spine
- large eyes
- live in the sea

Arachnids
- 80,000 species
- body divided into two main parts
- four pairs of legs
- jaws with fangs
- most are land-living

Centipedes
- 3,000 species
- body long and flattened
- one pair of legs per body segment
- long feelers
- jaws with fangs
- run fast
- live on land

Millipedes
- 10,000 species
- body long and rounded
- two pairs of legs per body segment
- short feelers
- walk slowly
- live on land

THE CUTICLE

An arthropod's cuticle is like a thick, stiff outermost layer of the skin. It forms a rigid casing, the exoskeleton, to support the soft inner parts of the body.

- waxy coating
- pore (hole) for wax
- inner cuticle
- wax gland
- touch-sensitive bristle
- outer cuticle
- skin
- nerve fibre

BEETLES AND WEEVILS

BEETLES AND THEIR SMALLER COUSINS, WEEVILS, MAKE UP THE LARGEST SUB-GROUP OF INSECTS. They are called the Coleoptera. There are almost half a million known kinds, or species, of coleopterans, making up about one third of all animal species. And hundreds of new species are found each year. Most insects have two pairs of wings, but in beetles the front two have become hard and strong, like a shield over the top of the body. They are called wing cases, or elytra. The wing cases form a protective covering for the delicate second pair of wings. These are folded under the wing cases when the beetle is at rest. As it takes off, the beetle lifts the hard wing cases and then unfurls its thin wings, which it flaps to fly away. Beetles are the most widespread of all insects. They live in almost every habitat and region of our planet except the sea. Some are almost microscopic, others are nearly as big as a fist.

◪ The great diving beetle must come to the surface every few minutes to gather air to breathe. It has strong mouthparts and can bite hard.

STRONGEST... !
The strongest insect is the rhinoceros beetle, also called the hercules beetle. It can lift and support more than 800 times its own weight.

◪ A typical weevil has a long trunk-like snout. Some weevils are pests, eating wheat and flour, or crops such as apples, carrots, nuts and clover.

Beetles are not only incredibly numerous, they are also extremely varied. The familiar red spotted ladybirds that we see in parks and gardens are brightly coloured to warn other animals that they taste horrible. Predators such as birds soon learn to avoid these small beetles.

Tiger and ground beetles are active hunters, with large eyes for seeing prey and long legs for racing after it. One kind of green ground beetle, the bombardier, can squirt a spray of stinging chemicals from its rear end at an attacker.

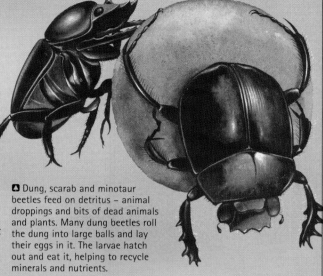

Dung, scarab and minotaur beetles feed on detritus – animal droppings and bits of dead animals and plants. Many dung beetles roll the dung into large balls and lay their eggs in it. The larvae hatch out and eat it, helping to recycle minerals and nutrients.

WEEVILS
Weevils form the largest sub-group of beetles, with more than 60,000 species. They feed on seeds, fruits and flowers. A weevil has a long, curved snout (called the rostrum), which looks like a tiny elephant's trunk.

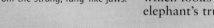

Green tiger beetles are truly the tigers of the insect world. They stalk and then rush after victims, killing them with a bite from the strong, fang-like jaws.

The surface of the wood is marked with their small, round flight holes, and inside is a network of tunnels and powdered wood. The larvae of longhorn and deathwatch beetles also tunnel through wood, eating and weakening it as they go.

NIGHT LIGHTS
On hot summer nights, flashes of pale green or yellow light can sometimes be seen among trees, or on the forest floor. These are fireflies and glow worms. They are not flies or worms, but kinds of beetle. Fireflies flash to attract each other in the mating season. Their wormlike larvae also give off light, to warn predators such as shrews that they have a nasty taste and should be left alone.

Old beams and other wooden objects often have round holes we call woodworm. These are the work of the furniture beetle. The adult beetles lay their eggs on wood (trees or furniture). When the larvae hatch from the eggs, they tunnel into the wood, feeding on it as they go. These larvae change into adults, which eat their way out and fly away.

Female fireflies and glow -worms have no wings and small wing cases, showing the segmented main body or abdomen underneath. The males are much smaller and fly to the females.

NATURE'S UNDERTAKERS
Sexton or burying beetles are the undertakers of the natural world. They have a keen sense of smell and are attracted to rotting bodies, such as dead birds or small mammals such as mice and rats. First the beetles mate, then they set to work to bury the corpse, by digging out the soil beneath it. They then lay their eggs in a chamber dug into the soil next to the body. When the larvae hatch, they feed on the decaying flesh of the corpse.

HEAVIEST... !
The heaviest insect is a kind of beetle, the goliath beetle of Africa. It can weigh up to 108 g, which is almost as heavy as two ordinary hen's eggs.

WATER BEETLES
Some beetles live in fresh water. Diving beetles use their hairy legs as oars to row themselves through the water. The larva of the great diving beetle is a fierce predator, catching tadpoles and small fish with its sharp, curved jaws. Whirligig beetles swirl about like tiny wind-up toys on the surface of a pond. Each eye is divided into two parts. One part looks up into the air, the other down into the water.

Beetles and weevils
(Coleoptera)
• almost 500,000 species
• front wings are hard wing cases
• biting mouthparts to eat small animals or plant food
• most are active, fast runners

43

BUTTERFLIES AND MOTHS

AFTER THE BEETLES, THE SECOND LARGEST SUB-GROUP OF INSECTS IS THE BUTTERFLIES AND MOTHS, WITH ABOUT 175,000 SPECIES. They live wherever there are trees and flowers, being most numerous in tropical parts of the world. They are known as Lepidoptera, a name that means "scaly winged", because their large, papery wings are covered with tiny scales. The bright patterns on the wings are made by different colours and patterns of scales, like a living mosaic. There are a number of differences between moths and butterflies. Most moths are active at night; butterflies usually fly by day. Most moths are dull browns and greys; many butterflies are brightly coloured. Most moths have feathery feelers (antennae); butterflies have thin, club-ended feelers.

◪ The peacock butterfly has large patches on its wings that look like eyes and are called "eye spots". When the butterfly is in danger, it opens its wings to reveal the eyes, which frighten away predators.

◪ Clearwings are day-flying moths. They look more like butterflies, with their bright colours and slim bodies.

◪ Blue morpho butterfly

Butterflies and moths are insects which go through a drastic change in body shape as they grow up. This is called complete metamorphosis. The life cycle begins when an adult male and female mate, often flitting about in a courtship flight. The female usually lays her eggs on the food plant – the plant that the caterpillars will eat when they hatch. She places them carefully, either in groups or singly, on the undersides of leaves. For the brimstone butterfly (see the box, opposite), the caterpillars' food plant is buckthorn. In fact, caterpillars do little else except eat. After growing and moulting its skin several times, each caterpillar changes into an inactive, hard-cased chrysalis. This seems to rest for a few weeks, or even through the winter.

◪ A butterfly or moth, like this large white butterfly, has a long, tube-shaped mouth. This is normally coiled up under the head. To sip nectar from deep in a flower the butterfly straightens its mouth and uses it like a drinking straw to sip up the sugary fluid.

◗ Moths usually have hairy, plump bodies. The feathery antennae of a male moth can pick up the female's scent from more than 1 km away.

The outside of the chrysalis doesn't appear to change, but inside the body breaks up into a kind of thick, living soup. This re-forms into the wings, legs, feelers and other parts of an adult butterfly or moth. The adult emerges from the chrysalis case and flies away to search for its own food, usually the sweet, sugary fluid called nectar in flowers.

Some butterflies and moths migrate long distances as adults, to avoid dry or cold seasons and find more sheltered places. In North America, monarch or milkweed butterflies fly south in late summer from Canada to Mexico. This journey of more than 3,200 km can take up to four months. In southeast Australia, bogong moths shelter in caves in the cool uplands during the hot, dry summer, and return to the lowlands to breed in the autumn.

LARGEST... !
The giant agrippa moth has the biggest wingspan of any insect, up to 30 cm from tip to tip. The birdwing butterfly of New Guinea is second. Its wingspan is about 28 cm.

Butterflies and moths
(*Lepidoptera*)
• 175,000 species
• adults have four wings, often colourful
• adult has long, tubular mouth
• most feed on flowers
• larvae are leaf-eating caterpillars

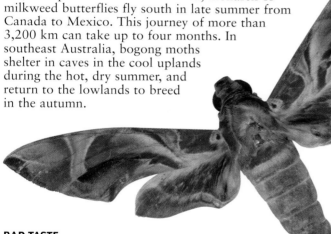

BAD TASTE

The bright colours of some butterflies and moths, especially in the caterpillar stage, warn animals who might try to eat them that they taste horrible. Others are brightly coloured to attract mates.

◗ A hawkmoth shown with its wings spread out

◗ The hawkmoths, like this elephant hawkmoth, are fast and powerful flyers with narrow, V-shaped wings.

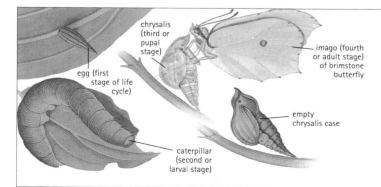

chrysalis (third or pupal stage)

imago (fourth or adult stage) of brimstone butterfly

egg (first stage of life cycle)

empty chrysalis case

caterpillar (second or larval stage)

THE LIFE CYCLE OF A BUTTERFLY

When a young butterfly or moth hatches from its egg, like this brimstone, it is a long, worm-shaped creature called a caterpillar, grub or larva. This crawls, eats and grows, moults its skin, eats and grows again, and so on, moulting perhaps seven times. Then it sheds its last skin, forms a hard case around itself and becomes an inactive chrysalis or pupa. Inside this case the creature's body undergoes amazing changes. Finally the adult butterfly emerges from the case, stretches its crumpled wings and flies away. These changes in body shape while growing up are called complete metamorphosis.

CRICKETS AND GRASSHOPPERS

CRICKETS AND GRASSHOPPERS HAVE LONG, POWERFUL BACK LEGS FOR LEAPING AND JUMPING, USUALLY TO ESCAPE PREDATORS.

Crickets, like this green bush cricket, and mantids usually live singly.

They belong to the insect sub-group known as Orthopterans. Most have camouflaged bodies, coloured and patterned to blend in with their surroundings. As they leap, they may spread their two rear wings in a flash of whirring colour. The young or larvae of crickets and grasshoppers look like small versions of the adult, except that they do not have wings. The wings grow gradually, each time the larva sheds its skin. This type of development is known as incomplete metamorphosis, and the larvae are called nymphs. There is no pupa or chrysalis stage (page 45). Other insects that grow like this include cockroaches, bugs, dragonflies, termites, mantids, earwigs and stoneflies.

Grasshoppers have large, fan-like rear wings. When these are not in use they are folded and protected by the smaller, harder front wings.

The rasping and chirping of crickets and grasshoppers are familiar sounds in hot weather. The male insects "sing" to warn others off their territory or to attract a mate. Crickets and the similar katydids rub the comb-like front wing veins together to make the noise. Grasshoppers and locusts rub their back legs against the front wing veins. Each leg has a row of hard pegs that make the wing vibrate. One kind of cricket, the mole cricket, lives in a burrow rather than on grass stems and plants like most crickets and grasshoppers. To make its song even louder, it digs a mating burrow with the entrance shaped like a double funnel.

A leaping desert locust straightens each leg section in turn.

The mole cricket's burrow entrance acts as a kind of loudspeaker. On a still night, its song can be heard more than a kilometre away.

STICK AND LEAF INSECTS
The stick and leaf insects, or phasmids, live mainly in tropical regions. They avoid birds and other predators with their amazing camouflage. Their bodies look like thin sticks or twigs, or like flat leaves.

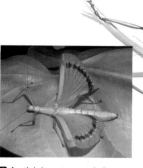

⬖ A stick insect spreads its large, fan-like rear wings.

Most of them are green or brown, to match the plants on which they feed. Some leaf insects even have V-shaped patterns on their bodies resembling the veins or ribs of a leaf. Others have brown edges, patches or blotches, so that they look like old or damaged leaves.

⬖ Leaf insects (shown here on the leaves) are extremely well camouflaged in both appearance and behaviour. They move and sway to mimic a leaf being blown by the wind. Stick insects (at the top) hold out their legs at the same angles as the twigs around them.

NO MALES NEEDED
Some kinds of female stick insect do not need to mate with a male before laying eggs. In some species males are hardly ever found. This kind of breeding is called parthenogenesis.

⬖ A grasshopper (left) has shorter antennae or feelers than a cricket (below).

MANTIDS
Mantids are fierce hunters. They catch and eat other small animals, such as large insects and spiders, grabbing them with their spiny, pincer-like front legs. The mantis has large eyes and excellent vision. It sits patiently on a plant or flower, waiting for a suitable victim to come near. Then it strikes, too fast for us to see, and grabs the prey in its spiny "arms". When some kinds of mantid breed, the female eats the male just after they mate, or even while mating. In other species there are no males. The females reproduce by parthenogenesis.

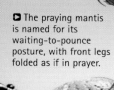

⬖ The praying mantis is named for its waiting-to-pounce posture, with front legs folded as if in prayer.

Crickets, locusts and grasshoppers
(Orthoptera)
• 20,500 species
• long, strong hind legs for jumping
• small, hard front wings
• large, fan-like rear wings
• feed on plants

Stick and leaf insects
(Phasmatoidea)
• 2,500 species
• live mainly in the tropics
• resemble leaves, twigs or sticks

• even the eggs are camouflaged, to resemble plant seeds
• large, fan-like rear wings
• eat plants

Mantids
(Mantodea)
• 1,800 species
• live mainly in warmer countries
• triangular head with big eyes
• large front legs with pincer-like claws
• eat mainly other insects

CRABS, LOBSTERS AND SHRIMPS

INSECTS ARE THE MOST COMMON ANIMALS ON LAND. But they do not live in salty water. Instead, another group of arthropods occupies the oceans – the crustaceans. They include crabs, lobsters, shrimps and barnacles. The shrimp-like krill eaten by great whales are crustaceans. So are the small creatures called copepods, which teem in such vast swarms that they are the most numerous animals in the sea. Some crustaceans, such as water fleas and crayfish, live in fresh water. A few, like woodlice, live on land.

◙ Common shore crab

◙ Like all crustaceans, the slipper lobster grows by shedding or moulting its old carapace (shell). The new one underneath enlarges and then hardens.

For many people, the most familiar crustaceans are crabs. There are thousands of crab species, from giant spider crabs with pincers as long as your arm, to tiny porcelain and pea crabs that would fit in this o. A typical crab has a flattened body covered by the hard, shell-like carapace. The abdomen (rear part of the body) is small and tucked under the shell at the back. There are ten limbs – one pair of large pincers and four pairs of walking legs. Most crabs live in the sea, but a few dwell in rivers and lakes. The common shore crab is very hardy and can live in both salt and fresh water, and even out of water for a few hours.

THE HERMIT'S HOME

The front end of a hermit crab has the typical hard crab carapace and pincers, and two pairs of large walking legs. But the rear of its body is soft and twisted. This is because a hermit crab lives in the abandoned shell of a sea snail, such as a whelk. It holds the shell from inside with its two pairs of smaller rear legs. When the hermit crab grows too big for its shell, it has to "move house". It finds a larger shell, and quickly slides its body backwards into the new home.

CRAYFISH AND LOBSTERS

Crayfish and lobsters are like elongated crabs with the rear body part, the abdomen, held out straight at the rear like a tail, rather than tucked underneath.

◙ The red-banded cleaner shrimp lives on coral reefs. Its bright colours advertise the service it provides – picking tiny parasites and pests off larger animals such as fish. The shrimp gets a meal and the fish gets cleaned.

◙ Krill live in cool oceans, in swarms several kilometres long, numbering many millions. They are cousins of shrimps and feed by filtering the tiny plankton from seawater.

The middle body part of crayfish and lobsters, the thorax, has four pairs of walking legs with a pair of very large, strong pincers or claws at the front. In some types of lobster one pincer is bigger and designed for crushing, while the smaller one is sharper for cutting and snipping.

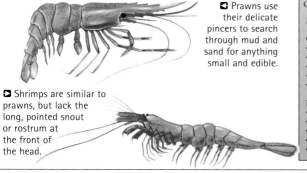

The lobster's head has two pairs of antennae. The larger pair curl out in front and may be longer than the whole body. The lobster uses these to feel among rocks for food such as shellfish, which it crushes with its pincers. A lobster is well protected. Its head and thorax are covered by a thick, rigid carapace. The abdomen has a series of jointed plates, one for each segment. It can also defend itself with its powerful pincers.

◑ Crayfish are the largest freshwater crustaceans. Like their cousins, lobsters, they feed at night. By day they hide in a lair, in a hole or under a stone.

SHRIMPS AND PRAWNS

Shrimps and prawns are like small, lightly built lobsters. Shrimps can crawl well but prawns usually swim by rowing with the five pairs of paddle-shaped limbs under the abdomen. The shrimp has a body flattened from top to bottom, while the prawn is flattened from side to side. They eat anything they can find, including dead animals. When alive they are almost transparent and well camouflaged against the rocks and sand. They only turn pink when cooked!

BIGGEST... !
The Japanese giant spider crab is the largest crustacean and the largest living arthropod. Its body is the size of a dinner plate, and it can measure 3.5 m across its outstretched claws.

◑ Some crabs, like the robber crab, live partly on land. This powerful crustacean can even climb up trees near the shore.

◑ Prawns use their delicate pincers to search through mud and sand for anything small and edible.

◑ Shrimps are similar to prawns, but lack the long, pointed snout or rostrum at the front of the head.

CRUSTACEANS

Main groups include:

Crabs
• 5,700 species
• most live in the sea
• round, flattened body, hard shell
• four pairs of walking legs
• one pair of pincers

Lobsters and crayfish
• 400 species
• most live in the sea
• long body
• four pairs of walking legs
• one pair of pincers

Shrimps and prawns
• 2,000 species
• most live in the sea
• long body
• swim and crawl well

All of the above are in the main crustacean group Decapoda, meaning "ten-limbed".

Krill
• 90 species
• swim in the open sea
• resemble shrimps
• live in gigantic shoals

SPIDERS

SPIDERS ARE MEMBERS OF THE ARTHROPOD GROUP CALLED ARACHNIDS. The main feature of an arachnid is that it has eight legs, unlike an insect which has six, and a crustacean which has ten or more. Other arachnids include harvestmen, scorpions, ticks and mites. With some 80,000 species, arachnids form the second largest group of arthropods, after insects. Like insects, they are mostly land-living, although a few kinds of spiders and mites inhabit fresh water. Unlike insects, they lack wings. Most arachnids are predators or hunters, but some mites and ticks are parasites of other animals. Arachnids live all over the world, in a wide range of habitats.

◪ Tarantula

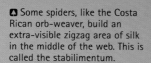

◪ Some spiders, like the Costa Rican orb-weaver, build an extra-visible zigzag area of silk in the middle of the web. This is called the stabilimentum.

Spiders have one important ability that sets them apart from most other arthropods, including other arachnids. They make a kind of silk thread using special parts at the rear of the body, called spinnerets. Spider silk is used for various purposes – to spin protective cocoons around the eggs, to make a parachute for a baby spider so that it can blow in the wind to a new place, to act as a safety line in case the spider loses its footing and falls, to line a burrow or tunnel, to wrap up and subdue prey before it is eaten, and to weave webs for catching prey.

◪ Bird-eating spiders have ver large mouthparts, or chelicerae with sharp fangs. They also have long palps (which loo like a front pair of legs) fo touching and tasting

◪ Huntsman spiders live in tropical forests. They are large and strong enough to catch prey by force, and do not spin webs.

Spider silk is one of the strongest materials known. It can take more strain than a steel thread of the same thickness. Different sorts of silk are used for different purposes. Cocoon silk is thick and smooth, while web silk is like sticky, coiled elastic.

HIDDEN DANGER

Trapdoor spiders live in burrows, using their silk to make a hinged, door-like covering to the entrance. The trapdoor spider detects vibrations in the ground as a suitable small creature passes by. Or it lays silk threads as tripwires that the creature touches. The spider then darts out of its burrow and bites the victim with its large fangs, which all spiders possess. It injects poison and drags its meal down into the burrow, closing the trapdoor behind.

MAKING A WEB

A common type of web is the orb web. It is roughly circular with radial threads like spokes in a wheel. First, the spider must choose a suitable place with twigs the correct distance apart. The spider sets out the top frame and makes a couple of radial threads (1). Next comes the rest of the frame and more radial threads (2), then the last of the spoke-like radials (3). These are all made from a strong, tight, non-sticky type of silk. The spider then works around in a spiral from the outside towards the centre, spinning a much looser, elastic, sticky silk to snare its prey (4).

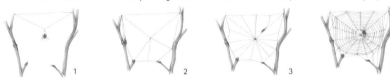

1   2   3   4

LARGEST... !
The largest spider is the goliath bird-eating spider, <u>Theraphosa leblondi</u>, of South America. It measures 28 cm across its legs. It catches other spiders, and also lizards, birds and small mammals like mice!

◱ This yellow agriope orb-web spider has wrapped a moth in silk thread to eat later. If the spider has plenty of food, it may leave the victim tied up but alive, hidden in the fork of a nearby twig.

WEBS GALORE

Web-spinning spiders make all shapes and sizes of webs. Some are woven in amazingly precise geometric patterns. Others are a tangle of threads in a dark corner. But when a victim hits the web, the silk threads quickly entangle it. If the web is badly damaged, the spider eats the silk and recycles it to spin another one.

POISONOUS SPIDERS

All spiders have poisonous bites. But only about 30 species have fangs strong enough, and poison powerful enough, to harm people. The most deadly are the black widows, Latrodectus, that live in many warm countries, the Australian funnel-web spiders and the Brazilian huntsman.

◱ The net-casting spider spins a small web and holds it out with its three front pairs of legs. The web is a net ready to throw over the prey. This spider's huge eyes watch for victims and see where to cast the net.

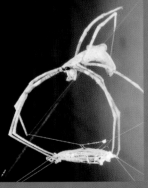

◱ Wolf spiders do not make webs. They run quickly across soil, rocks and tree bark after their prey, using their extra-long legs. Since they have no home base, the female wolf spider carries her whitish silk egg cocoon under her body.

ARACHNIDS

- members of the arthropod group
- about 80,000 species
- adult has eight legs

Spiders
- 50,000 species
- worldwide, all habitats
- body has obvious waist
- make webs from silk

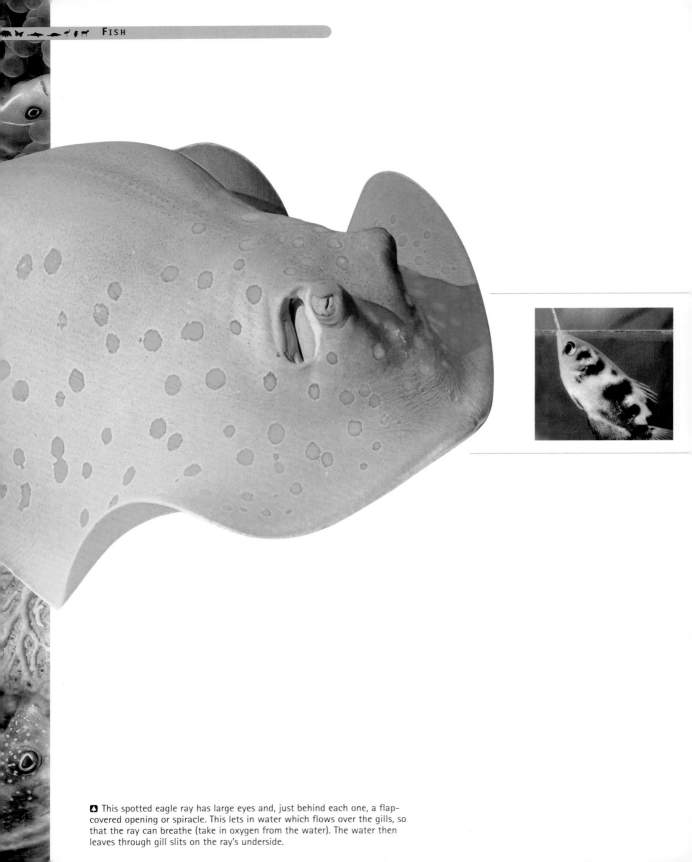

◩ This spotted eagle ray has large eyes and, just behind each one, a flap-covered opening or spiracle. This lets in water which flows over the gills, so that the ray can breathe (take in oxygen from the water). The water then leaves through gill slits on the ray's underside.

SECTION 4
FISH

FISH ARE EASY TO IDENTIFY. They live in water, breathe through their gills, are covered by shiny scales and swim by swishing their fins and tail. But there are exceptions. Lungfish can live out of water and breathe air. Some eels have no scales. Lampreys and hagfish, and some types of ray, have no fins or tail. But fish, like all other vertebrates, have an inner skeleton with a backbone.

Fish make up a vast and varied group. Their habitats range from the deepest oceans to the clearest mountain streams, from sunlit tropical lagoons to dark, chilly underground lakes. They have a greater size range than almost any other animal group, from dwarf gobies that could fit onto your little fingernail, to massive whale sharks as big as a truck. Fish are almost every shape and colour imaginable, from sharp-nosed, super-streamlined swordfish and marlin, to enormously bulky groupers, snake-like eels, and flatfish that are just that.

Fish obtain food in varied and imaginative ways. Some nibble at seaweed. Others filter tiny bits of food from the water. Sharks are the ultimate razor-toothed predators. Anglerfish use a "rod and line" made from their own bodies to catch their meals – of other fish!

WHAT ARE FISH?

World Watch

The activities of humans are putting ever more fish species at risk. Some, such as cod, are victims of overfishing – we simply catch too many. Others suffer because we pollute their waters, divert or build dams across their rivers, or take too much water for our own use. We also take fish species to new areas, on purpose or by accident. The large, predatory Nile perch (page 64) was introduced into Africa's Lake Victoria in the early 1960s. It has now eaten many of the lake's own cichlid fish and completely upset the natural balance of life there.

FISH ARE VERTEBRATES (ANIMALS WITH BACKBONES) THAT ARE COLD-BLOODED, LIVE IN WATER, BREATHE BY GILLS, SWIM WITH FINS AND A TAIL, AND HAVE A BODY COVERING OF SCALES. At least, this is true of most fish (page 53). Fish make up by far the largest group of vertebrate animals. There are some 24,000 species, which is more than all other vertebrate animals – amphibians, reptiles, birds and mammals – combined. The first fish to evolve on Earth, some 470 million years ago, were jawless fish. They had sucker-like mouths, rather than biting jaws with teeth. Two small groups, the lampreys and hagfish, survive today. A larger sub-group of fish is the sharks, rays and chimaeras. These are known as cartilaginous fish because they have a "backbone", or vertebral column, made of tough, gristly cartilage rather than true bone. Easily the largest fish sub-group is the bony fish, with skeletons of true bone – as people know if they get the bones stuck when they eat fish. Fish are extremely important as food in many parts of the world.

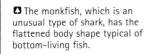
The monkfish, which is an unusual type of shark, has the flattened body shape typical of bottom-living fish.

◄ The red-spotted hawkfish is an alert and agile fish of shallow tropical waters around coral reefs.

All animals need oxygen to live. We breathe oxygen gas from the air into our lungs. A fish takes in oxygen dissolved in the water through gills on either side of its head. Most fish have four sets of gills, which are red and feathery. They are made of rows of lamellae, flat, delicate structures, filled with blood. Water flows into the fish's mouth and over the gills, where oxygen passes through the gill coverings into the blood, to be carried around the body. In sharks and other cartilaginous fish, the water then flows to the outside of the body through gill slits. In bony fish, the gills are covered by a bony flap, the operculum or gill cover, with a single slit along its rear edge.

◄ This scene shows members from all the main fish sub-groups. In the centre is a large cartilaginous fish – a wobbegong or carpet shark. It lurks on the sea bed, disguised as a rock. On the lower right is a chimaera, another type of cartilaginous fish. The eel-like creature just above the "wobby" is a lamprey, a jawless fish with a sucker mouth. On the far left three hagfish, also jawless, suck rotting flesh from a carcass. The large silvery fish, upper left, is a tarpon, a type of bony fish.

INSIDE A FISH

A typical fish like the salmon has a body that is mainly blocks of muscle, arranged in a zigzag pattern along either side of the backbone. These pull the backbone from side to side to swish the tail and make the fish swim.

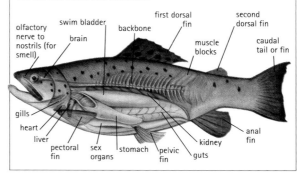

olfactory nerve to nostrils (for smell), swim bladder, brain, backbone, first dorsal fin, second dorsal fin, muscle blocks, caudal tail or fin, gills, heart, liver, pectoral fin, sex organs, stomach, pelvic fin, guts, kidney, anal fin

JAWLESS FISH

Jawless fish have a skeleton made of cartilage, not bone. They also have no side fins, no scales on the long, thin body, round gill openings and a sucking, disc- or funnel-shaped mouth. These creatures are survivors from a very early stage in the evolution of fish. They are mostly scavengers or parasites, sucking the blood of other water creatures.

 ◄ The common spotted dogfish is one of the smallest sharks.

FISH FINS

Fish have two kinds of fins. These are paired fins, usually somewhere along the sides of the body, and unpaired fins, which are generally the dorsal fins on the top or back, and the anal fins on the underside or belly. The unpaired fins help the fish to swim straight or lean to one side. The tail or caudal fin is also unpaired and provides the main thrust for swimming. The paired fins are the pectoral fins just behind the head and the pelvic fins, usually lower and to the rear. They help the fish turn sideways, slow down and even swim backwards.

FISH (Pisces)

• 24,000 species
• most have gills, fins, a tail, and a body covered with scales

Hagfish (Myxini)
• about 50 species
• eel-like body
• sucker-like mouth (no jaws)
• live in the sea

Lampreys (Cephalaspidomorphi)
• about 38 species
• eel-like body
• sucker-like mouth (no jaws)

• live in the sea and fresh water

Sharks and rays (Chondrichthyes)
• about 900 species
• skeleton of cartilage
• no gill flap over gill slits
• most live in the sea
• includes sharks, dogfish, sawfish, rays, skates

Bony fish (Osteichthyes)
• over 23,000 species
• skeleton of bone
• gill slits covered by gill flap
• live in the sea and fresh water
• includes vast majority of fish

SHARKS AND RAYS

SHARKS AND RAYS, AND THE CREATURES CALLED RATFISH OR CHIMAERAS, MAKE UP THE GROUP CALLED CARTILAGINOUS FISH. Their skeletons are not made of bone, as in other fish, but of cartilage – a gristly substance that is tough, yet light and bendy. The typical shark has a long, streamlined body. It is propelled by a tail with an upper lobe that is usually larger than the lower lobe. The shark's mouth is set back from the snout tip and is full of sharp teeth. The skin is not covered with the usual fish scales, but with tiny pointed structures called dermal denticles. These are much smaller versions of the teeth in the mouth. If you stroke shark skin the wrong way, from tail to head, the dermal denticles make the skin feel so rough that it could cause your hand to bleed.

A "mermaid's purse" washed up on a shore is the empty case in which a baby shark or ray developed. It attaches to rocks or weeds by the long, stringy tendrils.

A typical ratfish has a large head, big eyes, fleshy lips, sharp teeth, a long, tapering body and a "rat's tail" instead of the usual tail fins.

The largest predatory or hunting shark is the great white or white pointer, feared in all warmer oceans of the world. It can grow more than 6 m long.

Most sharks are fast-moving, torpedo-shaped hunters of the open ocean. But others, such as the carpet sharks or wobbegongs, have a flattened body shape. They also have fringes and tassels of skin to camouflage their bodies as seaweed-covered rocks. They spend much of their lives lying on the sea bed, waiting to ambush and gulp down any prey that comes near.

This spotted eagle ray has large eyes and, just behind each one, a flap-covered opening or spiracle. This lets in water which flows over the gills, so that the ray can breathe (take in oxygen from the water). The water then leaves through gill slits on the ray's underside.

World Watch

Every year around the world, 30–50 people are reported as killed by sharks. Also every year, about 100 million sharks are killed by people. They are caught for many reasons – for food, for sport by anglers, because their body parts are thought to have healing powers, and because they might menace tourist areas. Several kinds, including the great white, are now very rare. Some are protected by world wildlife laws.

FLYING THROUGH THE WATER

Most rays also have a body flattened from top to bottom. Their wide, flap-like pectoral fins look and work like a bird's wings. The ray flaps or undulates them to "fly" through the water. The majority of rays have wide, flattened, crunching teeth and feed on shellfish and worms that they uncover on the sea bed.

◆ The Caribbean reef shark, or black-tip cruises along the edges of coral reefs in its search for sick or injured fish, seals, seabirds and other likely victims.

POISON FOR DEFENCE

Chimaeras, the fish group also known as ratfish, usually live on or near the sea bed. They can live at great depths of more than 2,000 m. Most chimaeras have long, scale-less bodies. The ratfish (short-nose and long-nose chimaeras) have stringy, rat-like tails. Ploughnose chimaeras have a tail similar to that of a shark. All chimaeras have a long spine at the front of the dorsal (back) fin. This is linked to a venom gland. The poison in the spine can cause a painful wound to an attacker. Most chimaeras eat small sea-bottom creatures such as crabs, clams and shrimps, as well as other fish.

MAKING BABY SHARKS

Different sharks and rays have different ways of producing young. Some, such as the horned or Port Jackson sharks and the dogfish, lay eggs protected by tough, leathery cases. The mother hides these in seaweed or rocks. The youngster develops inside for several weeks, nourished by its large yolk sac, until it is ready to hatch and fend for itself. Others, such as the tiger sharks, produce eggs with thin shells that are kept inside the mother's body. The young feed from their yolk sacs, hatch from the thin shells and are then born. More extraordinary still are the hammerheads, blues, white-tips and bull sharks. The young grow inside the mother, but not inside egg shells. When their yolk is used up, they are nourished directly from the mother's blood. Finally they are born as well-formed young.

BIGGEST... !

The largest fish in the world is the whale shark, at more than 13 m long. It is not a fierce hunter. It feeds by filtering the tiny plants and animals of the plankton from sea water.

Sharks
(Elasmobranchii)
• about 375 species
• all but a couple live in the sea
• includes hammerhead, dogfish, carpet shark, mako, great white

Rays
(Rajiformes)
• about 450 species
• most live in the sea
• includes electric ray, stingray, skate, manta

Chimaeras
(Chimaeriformes)
• about 30 species
• live in the sea
• includes ratfish, chimaera

◆ Most rays, like this southern ray, stay near the sea bed. Like sharks, they have dozens of tiny electricity-sensing pits on the head. These detect weak pulses of electricity from the muscles of buried prey animals, which the ray then digs out. To hide from predators, the ray buries itself in the sand.

CHARACINS, CARP AND CATFISH

THESE THREE GROUPS INCLUDE NEARLY A THIRD OF ALL FISH – MORE THAN 6,000 SPECIES. They vary widely in appearance, but most live in fresh water. The majority can detect sounds in water, by picking up sound waves in the swim bladder, which other fish cannot do so well. In addition, these fish have special alarm substances in the skin that are released into the water if the skin is damaged. When a fish is seized by a predator, the substance passes into the water, alerting other members of the species to escape.

◳ The many colours and shapes of goldfish have been bred over centuries from wild carp.

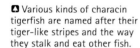

◳ Various kinds of characin tigerfish are named after their tiger-like stripes and the way they stalk and eat other fish.

Members of the carp group live across North America, Europe, northern Asia and Africa. They lack teeth in their jaws. Instead, they have a pair of toothed bones in the lower throat that they use to crush and grind food against a hardened pad at the base of the skull. Most carp eat a wide range of foods, including plants, fish and shellfish.

◳ The European catfish, or wels, is one of several kinds of catfish that grow to a massive size, reaching more than 1.8 m long.

Some types of carp, including the roach, bream, common and crucian carp, have been introduced to lakes and slow rivers around the world. They are caught by anglers and are popular as food. These types of carp are bottom feeders. They grub in the mud, using their sensitive whisker-like barbels to find worms, snails and shrimps.

AN UNUSUAL NURSERY

Most members of the carp group simply scatter their eggs in water and leave the young to hatch and fend for themselves. But the small carp, known as the bitterling, has a more unusual method. At the start of the breeding season the female develops a long egg-laying tube, the ovipositor.

⬆ Blue piranha

She uses this to place her eggs inside the shell of a freshwater mussel. The male bitterling releases his sperm near the mussel. As the mussel filter-feeds, the sperm are sucked in to fertilize the eggs.

⬇ Bream

One piranha cannot do much harm. But a large school of them can strip the flesh from a large animal like a horse in minutes. Piranhas are attracted by blood in the water. So a wounded animal that comes to drink at the river is in real danger.

⬆ The electric eel is shaped like an eel, but it is really a type of knifefish. It grows more than 2 m long and can give a 550-volt electric shock.

⬆ The neon tetra's colours are so bright, they seem to glow like electric neon lights.

⬇ Glassfish, types of small carp, form large schools. Like most carp, they feed at night.

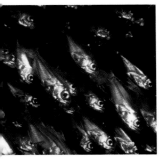

CHARACINS
The characins live in rivers and lakes in Central and South America and Africa. They include the piranhas of South America, and the tetras that have been bred in many colours as popular aquarium fish. Some characins eat plants, others eat small creatures such as insects and worms, and still others are hunters of larger animals such as fish and frogs. One group, the toothless characins, survive by sucking up the slime that covers leaves, stones and other underwater objects.

CAT'S WHISKERS
Catfish are named for the very long, whisker-like barbels around the mouth. The fleshy barbels taste the water to find food. Most catfish also have stiff spines at the front of the dorsal and pectoral fins. These can be "locked" in position, sticking outwards, so the fish is hard to swallow.

SHOCKING FISH
Knifefish are close relatives of catfish. They have special muscles that can produce pulses of electricity in the surrounding water. These pulses help them to find their way in muddy, dark lakes and rivers. The knifefish that produces the most powerful electrical pulses is the electric eel of northern South America. The electricity is so strong, it can stun prey fish. Another amazing catfish is the walking catfish. It can crawl on land, using its strong pectoral fins, and breathe air while it does so.

Carp (Cypriniformes)
• about 2,050 species
• almost all live in fresh water
• includes goldfish, loach, minnow, tench, barbel, mahseer

Characins (Charciformes)
• about 1,400 species
• live in fresh water
• includes pike characin, tetra, piranha, pacu, giant tigerfish

Catfish and knifefish (Siluriformes)
• about 2,415 species
• most live in fresh water
• includes wels, walking catfish, knifefish, butterfish, electric eel

NOT ALL SO FIERCE
The piranhas of South America have a fearsome reputation as bloodthirsty hunters. But some types of piranha, such as the pacu, feed on plants. The flesh-eating types include the red piranha. They are only about 30 cm long, but they have strong jaws and razor-sharp teeth for slicing chunks of flesh out of their victims.

⬆ The mirror carp has shiny, extra-large scales.

⬇ A female bitterling lays her eggs into a mussel, and the male waits to fertilize them. The baby fish emerge about 2–3 weeks later.

SCORPIONFISH AND SEAHORSES

SCORPIONFISH RANGE IN SHAPE FROM LONG AND SLENDER TO ALMOST AS ROUND AS BALLOONS. Most have spines, especially on the head and fins. Some, including the lionfish and stonefish, are extremely dangerous because the venom from their spines can kill people. Scorpionfish are all predators, catching other fish and shellfish. The pipefish and seahorse group is also extremely varied in shape, but most of the members have long, tube-shaped snouts. They live in warm, shallow waters near the coast. This group includes seadragons, shrimpfish, sea moths and trumpetfish. There is also a fish called the tubesnout, with a tubular snout, but it is in yet another fish group – the sticklebacks. They are found in rivers and lakes in northern continents and in the Atlantic and Pacific Oceans. Sticklebacks get their name from the strong, prickle-like spines on their backs.

◭ The lionfish has lacy, fan-shaped fins. These look delicate, but their spines jab deadly poison.

The scorpionfish's lumpy, mottled body is difficult to see as it lies among stones on the sea bed, watching for prey. Sharp spines in its dorsal and pelvic fins are linked to venom glands and can cause serious wounds. Its close relative, the lionfish, is far easier to see, with its bright colours, fan-like fins and lazy swimming. These features warn other creatures that the lionfish has deadly poison in its fin spines.

SUCKERED TO THE ROCKS

The lumpsucker, a relative of the scorpionfish, has a sucking disc on its throat formed from its pelvic fins. With this disc, the fish clings onto rocks in the shallows, to avoid being battered by waves. The small, dark eggs of lumpsuckers are sold as a type of caviar.

FATHER GIVES BIRTH

The seahorse does not lay eggs, but seems to give birth to its baby fish – and it is not the female that does this, but the male! The female seahorse lays her eggs into a special pouch on the male's front. He keeps the eggs safe here while they hatch and grow.

◭ The stonefish lies in shallow water, among weed and rocks, or part-buried in sand. People sometimes accidentally step on it when wading along a beach. The small spines on its back contain one of the most powerful venoms in the animal kingdom.

◨ Seahorses use their curly tails to hang onto coral branches or seaweed fronds. They swim slowly by rapidly flapping the dorsal fin on the back.

◪ The flying gurnard of the Atlantic Ocean has enormous pectoral fins, like wide wings. But this fish cannot fly, or even glide like the flyingfish.

The male seahorse even nourishes the tiny babies with a special substance from his own body. When the young are ready for the outside world, they shoot out through the opening of the pouch. They quickly attach themselves to floating weed or other objects and, like their parents, feed on tiny animal plankton.

PIPEFISH

The pipefish has a pencil-sized body encased in bony armour plates. Like its cousin, the seahorse, it has a long snout but no teeth, and feeds by sucking in tiny animals from the plankton. Also like the seahorse, the male pipefish keeps or incubates the female's eggs in a pouch on his own body. The largest pipefish grow to about 50 cm long.

◪ Pipefish curve themselves into the shape of seaweed, for better camouflage.

CARING PARENT

The male three-spined stickleback takes good care of his young. He builds a nest from bits of water plants stuck together with sticky substances from his own body. He then "dances" to attract a female, swimming to show off his brightly coloured throat and underside. These have turned bright red for the breeding season. The female comes to the nest and lays her eggs, then the male fertilizes them. He stays at the nest and chases off intruders. When the fry (baby fish) hatch, he guards them for a few weeks, until they can fend for themselves.

male in breeding colours

nest

female

Scorpionfish
(Scorpaeniformes)
• about 1,200 species
• most live in the sea, some in fresh water
• includes stonefish, sea robin, sculpin, lionfish, lumpsucker, tub gurnard, sablefish

Seahorses and pipefish
(Sygnathiformes)
• about 275 species
• live in the sea and fresh water
• thin, tubular snout for sucking in food

Sticklebacks
(Gasterosteiformes)
• about 10 species
• live in the sea and fresh water
• includes three-, four-, nine-, and 15-spined sticklebacks

FLATFISH AND TRIGGERFISH

FLATFISH LIVE IN ALL THE WORLD'S OCEANS, EXCEPT IN POLAR REGIONS. There are a few species in fresh water. The body of a flatfish is extremely flattened from one side to the other. (Rays look similar, but their bodies are flattened from top to bottom.) The flatfish spends much of its life swimming or lying on one side on the sea bed.

Both its eyes are on the other side, facing upwards, so it can watch for prey and predators. Some flatfish have both eyes on the right side; others have them on the left. Many flatfish are also masters of camouflage. They change their coloration and pattern to match the surroundings, making them very hard to see. All flatfish are predators and feed on shellfish, worms and similar sea bed animals. The triggerfish group includes poisonous pufferfish, spiny porcupinefish that can puff up their bodies like balloons, and the giant ocean sunfish. In most of these fish the mouth and a few teeth form a structure like a bird's beak. Most live along tropical coasts near the sea bed.

⬛ Different types of pufferfish have vivid colours and patterns. They "puff" up by swallowing water, so becoming too big to be swallowed.

⬛ The peacock flounder has both eyes on the left body side. It also has a large, spiny dorsal fin that begins just below its mouth.

⬛ Ocean sunfish

When a baby flatfish first hatches from its egg, it has a normal fish-like body shape, with an eye on each side of its head. Over the next few weeks, one eye moves across the top of its head, so it is close to the other eye. At the same time the body becomes thin or flat and the mouth twists so that it lies on the same side as the two eyes. Turbots, some flounders, topknots, brill and the windowpane (an exceptionally flat flatfish) usually have both eyes on the left side, and so lie on the right or blind underside. Halibut, plaice, dab, other flounders and most soles are right-eyed. A resting flatfish usually flicks a little sand or gravel over its body, to conceal its fins and blur its outline for even better camouflage.

TASTY?! ⚠

Some pufferfish have extremely poisonous flesh, yet they are eaten as a delicacy, fugu, by people in some Asian countries. The fish are prepared by specially trained chefs, who know which body parts contain the poison.

⬛ The common flounder grows to about 50 cm long. It lies on its left side, unlike the summer, starry and peacock flounders.

BIGGEST FLATFISH

The Atlantic halibut is one of the biggest of all the flatfish, at 2.5 m long and 295 kg in weight. However, due to overfishing, halibut of this size are now rare. They are more active than most flatfish, and chase prey rather than just lying in wait on the sea floor. Halibut feed on other fish, as well as on squid and crustaceans such as shrimps.

◄ The cowfish is a type of triggerfish named for the two spines above its eyes, which look like a cow's horns.

TRIGGERFISH

Most triggerfish are brightly coloured and live around coral reefs. They are named for the special tilting spines of the first dorsal fin. The front, larger spine can be "locked" upright by the second spine just behind it, like cocking the trigger of a gun. When in danger, the triggerfish takes shelter in a crevice among the rocks and locks its strong spine in the upright position. It is then very difficult for a predator to attack and remove the triggerfish.

► Plaice, like most flatfish, have a pale or white underside. This is because it is rarely seen.

PUFFERS AND PORCUPINE SPINES

The slow-swimming porcupinefish grows to about 90 cm long and lives in warm coastal waters, where it feeds on prey such as sea urchins, starfish and shellfish. For protection, it is covered with large, sharp spines. Normally these lie flat against the body. But if threatened, the porcupinefish gulps in water to make its body swell in size, until it is almost round. This forces the spines to stand out, making the fish like a huge prickly beach ball.

SUNBATHING FISH

The amazing ocean sunfish is shaped like a huge pancake. It has tall, thin dorsal and anal fins, and a fleshy frill for a tail. This massive fish grows to 4 m long and weighs up to 2 tonnes. Ocean sunfish are rare and live far out at sea, eating jellyfish, comb-jellies and other soft-bodied creatures. The name comes from this fish's habit of lying on the sea's surface, as though it is sunbathing.

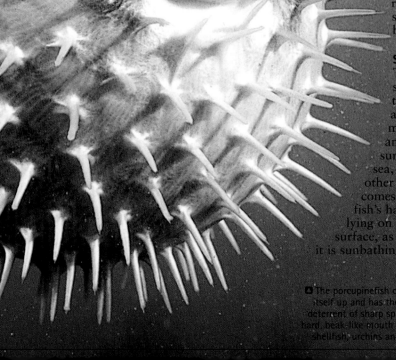

▲ The porcupinefish can puff itself up and has the added deterrent of sharp spines. Its hard, beak-like mouth crushes shellfish, urchins and crabs.

Flatfish
(Pleuronectiformes)
• about 540 species
• nearly all live in the sea
• includes sole, plaice, turbot, brill, tonguefish, adalah

Triggerfish
(Tetraodontiformes)
• about 350 species
• mostly sea-dwelling, some freshwater species
• includes boxfish, pufferfish, burrfish, cowfish, filefish

PERCH, GROUPERS AND DRUMS

THE HUGE GROUP OF PERCH-LIKE FISH, THE PERCIFORMS, CONTAINS MORE THAN 9,000 SPECIES – ALMOST HALF OF ALL KINDS OF FISH. They range from tiny gobies smaller than the word 'goby', to huge, strong, superfast, open-ocean predators such as marlin and barracudas, to ponderous, massive, vast-mouthed, heavy-bodied groupers. Perch-like fish live in all aquatic (watery) habitats, from rushing mountain streams to tropical coral reefs, icy polar seas and the ocean depths. Most have a front dorsal fin with spiny fin rays (the "rods" that hold up the soft fin parts). Some have a second dorsal fin too, but this has soft, bendy fin rays. There is also a spine at the front of each pelvic fin, and the pelvic fins are quite far forward on the body, below the pectoral fins.

◻ Archerfish are small, perch-like fish of tropical rivers, swamps, bays and estuaries. The archer gulps in a mouthful of water and squirts it hard from just under the surface at a small insect or similar target on a plant above. The victim is knocked into the water and gobbled up.

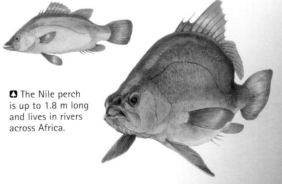

◻ The Nile perch is up to 1.8 m long and lives in rivers across Africa.

Groupers and seabass make up one of the biggest sea-dwelling families of perch-like fish. Most have robust, powerful bodies and two or three spines on the gill flap. Some seabasses and groupers, such as the striped bass and Nassau grouper, are important food fish and are caught in large numbers. The giant seabass of the Pacific North American coast grows to 1.8 m long. The jewfish is the largest member of the family. It can grow to more than 2.4 m long and weigh as much as 295 kg. It usually lives in shallow water close to the shore, where it preys on a range of creatures including fish, squid, crabs and shellfish.

and seize anything that comes near in their huge mouths. Dusk is the favourite hunting time. Groupers have been known to follow human divers, but attacks are rare.

AGGRESSIVE GROUPERS
Groupers are fierce hunters and usually ambush their prey. They hide among rocks

◻ A coney grouper, 30 cm long, watches from near its lair, a cave in a coral reef.

NOISY FISH
Another large group of perch-like fish is the drum and croaker family. Most live in shallow tropical seas. As their names suggest, these fish make a variety of sounds using special muscles to vibrate the swim bladder. The black drum of the western Atlantic Ocean grows to 1.8 m long and can weigh as much as 65 kg. The white seabass is also a type of drum, and about the same size.

◘ The Murray cod is a type of seabass, but it lives in lakes and rivers in eastern Australia. It may reach a length of 1.8 m.

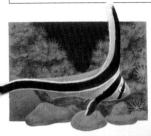

◘ Jack-knife drum fish

FAST DARTERS

The largest freshwater group of perch-like fish is the perch family itself, with more than 160 species living in North America, Europe and Asia. The perch, with its spiny dorsal fin and greenish dark-barred body, has been introduced to lakes and slow-flowing rivers in many parts of the world. Some members of this family are small, colourful fish called darters, which live along the beds of fast-moving streams in North America. Most are less than 10 cm long. The males are especially brightly coloured during the breeding season, when they swim and dart to attract female darters.

The male finds a nesting area among gravel on the stream bed, where the female lays her eggs. He fertilizes the eggs and guards them until they hatch.

The walleye is one of the largest in the perch family, at 90 cm long. It lives deep in large rivers and lakes, eating fish, frogs and insects. Newly hatched fry drift for a few days near the surface, nourished by their yolk sacs. Then they feed on plankton until they are big enough to catch fish.

SOME PERCH-LIKE GROUPS:

Perches (Percidae)
• about 160 species
• live in fresh water
• includes darters, ruffe, zander

Groupers and seabass (Serranidae)
• about 400 species
• most live in the sea
• includes jewfish, coney

Drums and croakers (Sciaenidae)
• about 270 species
• most live in the sea
• includes Atlantic croaker, jack-knife fish, red drum, black drum, red mullet, spotted seatrout

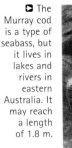

◘ The brown marbled grouper is one of several groupers that grows larger than an adult human. It can easily swallow prey up to 90 cm long, into its cavernous mouth.

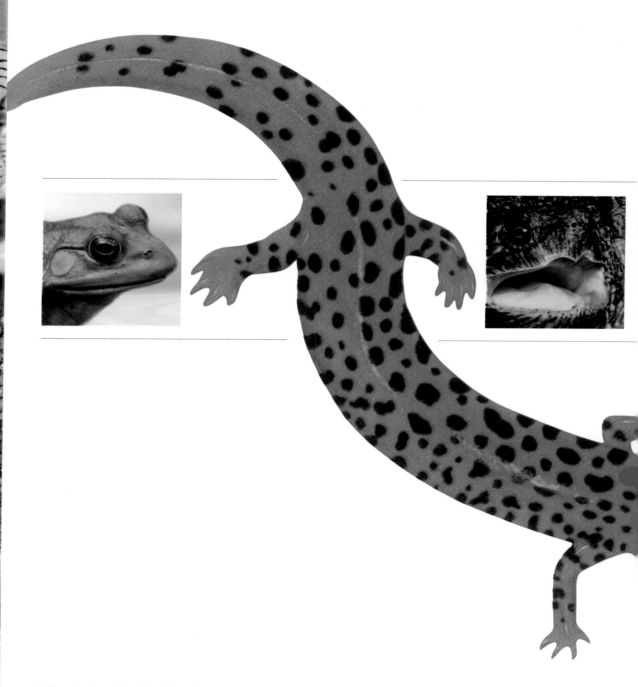

The red salamander of North America.

SECTION 5

AMPHIBIANS & REPTILES

AMPHIBIANS LIVE A STRANGE DOUBLE LIFE. Most begin as tiny black dots in little balls of jelly floating in water. These eggs, or spawn, hatch into tadpoles that breathe by gills and swim with their tails. But as they grow, tadpoles undergo an amazing change called metamorphosis. They lose their gills and tails, and develop lungs for breathing air and legs for hopping on land. They develop into adult frogs, toads, salamanders and newts.

Most amphibians have soft, moist skin. Reptiles do not. They can be recognized by their tough, scaly skin. The reptile group includes some of the most dangerous animals. There are poisonous snakes with deadly venom, such as cobras, rattlers and vipers. Constrictor snakes, like pythons and boas, squeeze the life from their victims. Crocodiles and alligators threaten enemies with their large, gaping mouths, equipped with rows of pointed teeth.

Turtles, tortoises and terrapins live a slow-paced life, safe in their domed protective shells. Much speedier are the lizards, another reptile sub-group. Some dart about so fast that we can hardly follow their movements. Lizards range in size from little geckos that make a big meal of a fly, to monitors, such as the Komodo dragon, that can devour a small goat.

WHAT ARE AMPHIBIANS?

AMPHIBIANS ARE COLD-BLOODED ANIMALS THAT HAVE A "DOUBLE LIFE". They begin in water, as jelly-covered eggs which hatch into tadpoles that breathe by gills and swim with their tails. The tadpoles change shape or metamorphose as they grow, into adults that breathe by lungs and walk on land on four legs. The 4,000 or so species live in all regions except Antarctica and the far north.

❍ The spring peeper frog is named for its "peep-peep" call.

❍ Some newts have frilly crests of skin along the back. At breeding time, the male's crest becomes larger and his body develops brighter colours.

Like fish and reptiles, amphibians are cold-blooded. Unlike birds and mammals, they cannot make body heat to keep themselves at a constant warm temperature. Their bodies are usually at about the same temperature as the air or water around them. When they are warm, they can move actively. But in cold conditions, they cannot. They become still and their body processes slow down. This is called torpor. In temperate regions, many amphibians are torpid or "asleep" in winter.

BIGGEST... !
The biggest amphibians are the giant salamanders of eastern Asia, especially China and Japan. They grow up to 1.5 m in total length.

AMPHIBIAN EGGS
An amphibian begins life as a small, dark, dot-like egg. This contains yolk for nourishment and is surrounded by several layers of jelly. It does not have a protective outer shell like a reptile egg, so it must be laid in water or moist surroundings, to prevent it drying out. Lots of jelly-covered eggs clustered together are known as spawn.

BREATHING IN WATER
The eggs grow and become comma-shaped, then hatch into larval amphibians – tadpoles. These have feathery gills on the sides of the head (external gills) for absorbing oxygen from the water. Most amphibians lose their gills when they become adults, and take in oxygen through their lungs and moist skin. But some, such as the mudpuppy, keep their gills.

GROUPS OF AMPHIBIANS
More species of amphibians are being discovered every year, especially in their main habitats, the tropical rainforests. There are three main kinds of amphibians. They are newts and salamanders, frogs and toads, and caecilians.

A typical newt or salamander has a long lizard-like body and tail.

❍ A frog leaps using its powerful back legs. Each section of the leg is larger than the one above it. So the thigh is shortest, then the shin, and the foot is the longest. The hip, knee and ankle joints straighten to fling the frog into the air.

FROZEN! ⚠
The spring peeper frog of North America can survive for as long as three days in icy temperatures, with almost half of the blood and other fluids in its body frozen solid. The frog produces extra glucose sugar, which concentrates its body fluids and reduces the amount of ice that forms, especially around its heart and brain.

◪ Many frogs have brightly coloured skin, like the tomato frog. Usually, the brighter they are, the more horrible-tasting the frog's flesh. The colours warn predators to leave the frog alone.

◪ Caecilians, also called apodans, have no legs. They live underground, feeding on grubs and worms, although a few dwell in ponds and streams. They are eyeless and find their prey by touch and smell. They also have small scales in their skin, like reptiles.

It has four usually small, sprawling legs at its sides, and smooth, scale-less skin. Most are active in the evening or at night, when they hunt for small creatures such as insects, spiders and worms. In fact, all amphibians are predators. They cannot chew so they gulp down their victims whole, often still alive and struggling.

◪ The axolotl is a strange salamander that keeps its feathery gills even when adult.

A typical frog or toad is in many ways the opposite of a salamander. It has a short, compact body, very long back legs for jumping, and no tail. The third amphibian group is the caecilians. These have no limbs at all and resemble overgrown earthworms. They burrow in the earth and dead leaves of tropical forests, searching for and devouring small soil creatures.

spawn (jelly-covered eggs)

tadpole (larva)

legs grow and tail shrinks in young adult

adult frog is tail-less

LIFE OF CHANGE
The lives of most amphibians start in water and move onto land. The drastic change in shape from legless tadpole to four-legged adult is known as metamorphosis. It takes about 3–4 months in the common frog.

AMPHIBIANS
- about 4,000 species
- vertebrates (animals with backbones)
- larvae or tadpoles live in water
- adults mostly live on land
- worldwide except coldest regions

Newts and salamanders (*Caudata*)
- about 360 species
- long body and tail, most four-legged

Frogs and toads (*Anura*)
- about 3,400 species
- no tail in adult
- long back legs for leaping

Caecilians (*Apoda*)
- about 160 species
- long worm-like body, no legs
- tropical and warm forests

◪ Bullfrogs are large, powerful frogs that eat a range of fish, insects, lizards, snakes, small mammals such as mice and other prey — including smaller frogs. There are bullfrog species in North America, South America and Africa.

FROGS AND TOADS

FROGS AND TOADS ARE BY FAR THE BIGGEST GROUP OF AMPHIBIANS, WITH MORE THAN 3,400 SPECIES. They live on all continents except Antarctica, and in habitats ranging from deserts

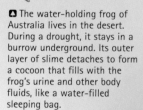

⬧ Surinam toad

to cold mountain streams. But they are most common in tropical and subtropical swamps and rainforests. The name "frog" was once used for the slender, smooth-skinned types that could leap well, and "toad" for the plump, rough-skinned species that prefer to waddle. Now both names are used for similar species and there is no clear difference between a frog and a toad.

⬧ Tree frogs have sucker-like disks at the ends of their toes.

All frogs and toads are tailless and have strong back legs for jumping. The front legs are smaller and cushion the landing. A frog's body is short, with a strong backbone to cope with the physical stresses of jumping, and there is no narrow neck between the head and body. The large eyes are usually on the top of the very wide-mouthed head, so the frog can still see when it is almost submerged in water.

SMALLEST... !
One of the smallest frogs in the world was discovered on the island of Cuba in 1997. It measures only 1 cm long. Its scientific name is *Eleutherodactylus iberia*.

A FROG'S LIFE CYCLE
A typical frog or toad lays its eggs in water. These hatch into tiny tadpoles with tails for swimming and fluffy gills for breathing in water. The young tadpole feeds on plants. As it grows, it loses its external gills and develops lungs in its chest for breathing air. It gradually loses its tail too, and develops legs. The head broadens, the body become short and thick, and the tadpole has metamorphosed into a froglet, ready to venture onto land.

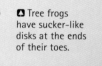

⬧ A frog pushes off with its toes, launching its small, streamlined body into a leap at least 10 times its own length.

⬧ The water-holding frog of Australia lives in the desert. During a drought, it stays in a burrow underground. Its outer layer of slime detaches to form a cocoon that fills with the frog's urine and other body fluids, like a water-filled sleeping bag.

⬧ In Central American rainforests, it is so damp that the strawberry poison-arrow frog can carry her tadpole on her back, without it drying out.

◻ The cane toad is also called the marine or giant toad. It was taken from South America to Australia, to eat beetle pests in sugar cane fields. But it prefers small creatures that are natural inhabitants in the area, making some of them very rare animals.

FROG CALLS

Male frogs and toads make loud calls to attract females. Each species has its own particular call, and the green frog can be heard hundreds of metres away. The calls of frogs are made louder in a vocal sac below the chin, as air from the lungs is forced over the vocal cords in the neck. Females do not usually make any sounds.

CARING FOR YOUNG

Some frogs do not leave their eggs in water to hatch, but carry them around to make sure they do not get eaten. As the female marsupial frog lays her eggs, the male fertilizes them and helps her pack them into a backpack-like skin pouch on her back, where they hatch and start to develop. After a few weeks the young hop into the water to complete their growth. The female Surinam toad carries her young in separate skin pouches on her back, until they are fully formed mini-toads.

POISONOUS FROGS

The bright colours of the poison-arrow (or arrow-poison) frogs warn other animals to stay away. Glands in the body release a strong venom into the frog's skin. Even a few drops of this can be lethal to a predator. Traditionally, local people in Central and South America tip their hunting arrows with this substance.

◻ Many frogs and toads make their calls louder by blowing up the chin skin like a balloon. The stretched skin vibrates or resonates to increase the volume of the sound.

The flying frog of Southeast Asia does not really fly, but spreads its huge webbed feet to glide 12 m from tree to tree.

SOME GROUPS OF FROGS AND TOADS (continued from page 69):

Ranid or "true" frogs (Ranidae)
• about 650 species
• slim, smooth-skinned body
• pointed head
• mostly live in water but some dwell in trees
• includes common frog, bullfrog

Bufid or "true" toads (Bufonidae)
• about 400 species
• stout body
• often rough, warty skin
• most live mainly on land
• includes cane toad, natterjack

Tree frogs (Hylidae)
• more than 770 species
• slender body
• long legs
• most live in trees
• webbed feet with sticky pads on disc-like toe-tips

Leptodactylid frogs (Leptodactylidae)
• more than 900 species
• varied body form
• land-living and water-living species
• includes horned frog, chirping frog

Narrow-mouthed frogs (Microhylidae)
• more than 320 species
• stout body
• small mouth
• live in burrows or trees
• includes rain frog

Poison-arrow (arrow-poison) frogs (Dendrobatidae)
• over 170 species
• mainly tropical rainforests
• slim, small body
• sticky discs on toes
• brightly coloured
• live on ground or in trees

USEFUL! ⚠

The poison fluid or secretion from poison-arrow frog skin may have medical uses. The secretions of the phantasmal poison-arrow frog are far more effective at stopping pain than the usual pain-killing drugs. Those of the golden poison-arrow frog may help patients who have had heart attacks.

◻ Green tree frogs are camouflaged among the leaves as they wait for their small insect prey. They can cling to twigs, wet glossy leaves and even window glass using the sucker-like discs on their toes.

WHAT ARE REPTILES?

REPTILES ARE ANIMALS WITH BACKBONES (VERTEBRATES) THAT ARE COLD-BLOODED, HAVE SCALES ON THEIR SKIN AND LAY EGGS (page 67). Most reptiles have four legs with five toes on each foot, but snakes have no limbs at all. Most reptiles live on land, but marine turtles and sea snakes stay in the sea, except to come ashore briefly and lay their eggs. Most reptile eggs have shells that are tough yet leathery and flexible, unlike the hard, brittle shells of birds' eggs. However, some snakes do not lay eggs, but give birth to babies.

◩ The pond slider is a common turtle in North, Central and South America. It rarely leaves the water.

The main groups of reptiles are the turtles and tortoises, the crocodiles and alligators, the lizards and the snakes. Most live on land, but many turtles and terrapins, also most crocodiles and alligators, and even some snakes, spend time in ponds, swamps and rivers. A few, including the saltwater crocodile, venture into the sea.

Reptiles may not seem to be social animals, in the way that birds form flocks or monkeys live in troops. Yet they have many ways of communicating, especially with others of their own species at mating time. Lizards bob their heads and show off their skin crests and brightly coloured patterns. Snakes leave chemical messages for their partners, which consist of scent-like substances called pheromones, produced in their bodies. Some reptiles, including crocodiles and geckos, make hisses, grunts and calls to attract mates.

THE REPTILE'S EGG
The leathery shell of a reptile egg gives protection and prevents it from drying out, even in the desert heat. Inside are layers of fluid to protect the developing embryo (unhatched baby), and yolk to provide it with nourishment.

🔲 Worm lizards are not worms or lizards, but reptiles that resemble large earthworms. They burrow in the soil of tropical forests.

◩ Hingeback tortoises can tilt down the rear of the shell to give extra protection to the back legs and tail.

SCALY! ⚠
The skin of a reptile is covered with hard scales. These are made of keratin, the same substance that forms our nails and hair. In some reptiles, such as crocodiles, the scales are strengthened by plates of bones, making a tough armour.

◀ The shell of a softshell turtle does not have ha‍ horny, strengthening plates, as in other turtles an‍ tortoises. So it feels slightly soft and rubbery.

When breeding, most female reptiles lay eggs and then leave these to develop and hatch on their own. But a few species, such as some skinks, pythons and crocodiles, guard their eggs and even the babies too, protecting them from enemies. Some snakes and lizards keep their developing eggs inside their bodies, where they hatch and the mother gives birth to the young.

⬆ Marine iguanas are some of the few reptiles that spend time in the sea. These large lizards dive to munch on seaweeds.

REPTILES	
• about 6,560 species • cold-blooded vertebrates • scaly skin • lay eggs • most have four legs • worldwide except polar regions	**Tuatara** *(Rhynchocephalia)* • 1 species • lizard-like, with head and back crest • only in New Zealand
Lizards *(Sauria)* • about 3,750 species • long, slim body, long tail • includes skinks, geckos, chameleons, iguanas, monitors	**Worm lizards** *(Amphisbaenia)* • about 140 species • long slender body, no limbs • includes worm lizards, shield snouts
Crocodiles *(Crocodilia)* • 22 species • long body armoured with thick scales, long tail • includes crocodiles, caimans, alligators, gharial	**Snakes** *(Serpentes)* • about 2,400 species • long worm-like body, no limbs • includes pythons, boas, vipers
	Turtles and tortoises *(Chelonia)* • about 250 species • body protected by a hard, domed shell • includes tortoises, terrapins, turtles

COLD BODIES

Reptiles are cold-blooded creatures. This means they cannot control their body temperatures themselves. They depend on the heat of the sun to become warm, so that they can be active and move about. In cold conditions, reptiles move slowly or not at all. This cold, immobile condition is known as torpor. One advantage of being cold-blooded is that reptiles do not need to use so much energy as warm-blooded animals, who must "burn" energy from their food to produce body heat. So reptiles need to eat far less food than warm-blooded birds and mammals of the same body size – perhaps only one-tenth of the amount.

⬇ Water dragons (below) are mostly large tropical lizards that swim well by lashing their tails from side to side. Caimans (right) are smaller members of the crocodile group from Central and South America. They grow to about 1.8 m long.

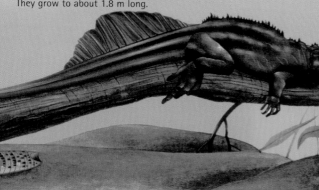

⬆ The spotted water snake lives in swamps and creeks in northern parts of Australia. Its nostrils are set high on its head, so it can take a breath without poking its whole head out of the water.

⬆ Most terrapins have wide feet with partly webbed toes, for efficient swimming.

TORTOISES, TURTLES AND TERRAPINS

THERE ARE ABOUT 250 SPECIES OF TURTLES, TORTOISES AND TERRAPINS, FOUND IN MOST WARM PARTS OF THE WORLD. They are easily recognized by the hard, rounded shell that protects the main part of the body. The mostly land-dwelling tortoises thrive in all kinds of habitats, including desert, woodland and mountains. Turtles and terrapins live chiefly in rivers and ponds. They are slow and ungainly on land, but swift in the water. (Marine turtles are a separate group.)

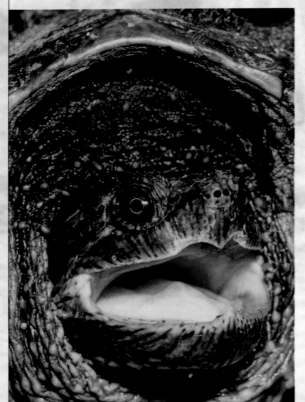

◙ The matamata is an extraordinary-looking turtle about 40 cm long from the Amazon region of South America. It has an arrow-shaped head and a very wide mouth, to gulp in fish and other water animals. Its tiny eyes are about halfway along the sides of the "arrow".

◙ Snapping turtles lurk in ponds and lakes from Canada, south through North to Central America. They grab any small animal as prey.

> ### OLD! ⚠
> Turtles are among the longest-lived of all animals. Box turtles of North America and spur-thighed tortoises in Europe survive to over 100 years old. A Marion's tortoise, taken from the Seychelles to Mauritius in 1766, lived until 1918. It died due to an accident – at least 152 years old.

Turtles, terrapins and tortoises are known as chelonians. They do not have teeth. Instead, a turtle or tortoise has a strong, beak-like mouth with hard ridges along the jaw edges for biting food. Many chelonians are predators, catching other animals to eat. Others, including many tortoises, are plant-eaters. They swallow each piece they bite since they cannot chew.

Turtles reproduce by laying eggs, usually in a hole in the ground. The female lays her eggs in a warm place and leaves them to incubate and hatch alone. The young receive no parental care.

THE TURTLE'S SHELL
The shell of a turtle or tortoise has two parts – the upper carapace and the lower plastron. Each part has two layers of plates like jigsaw puzzle pieces. These are made of bone on the inside, and horn on the outside like normal reptile scales. The outer plates are called scutes. The two parts meet at the sides, with openings for the turtle's head, legs and tail. The ribs and backbone are fixed to the upper inside of the carapace.

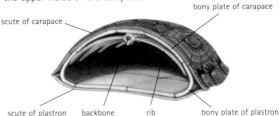

bony plate of carapace
scute of carapace
scute of plastron   backbone   rib   bony plate of plastron

◄ Wood turtles catch worms, insects and grubs, and can climb into bushes. They were once caught and kept as pets, but this has made them rare.

CAMOUFLAGED MATAMATA

Many turtles and tortoises are brownish or green, to blend with their surroundings of mud, leaves and waterweeds. This helps them to hide as they wait for prey to come near or stay unnoticed by predators. The matamata is a member of the snake-necked turtle family, and has most unusual camouflage. With its ridged shell and flattened head, fringed with flaps of skin, it looks like a clump of bark and leaves in the water. When a victim passes by, the matamata simply opens its large mouth. Water – and the prey – rush in. The turtle then closes its mouth, squeezes the water out at the sides and swallows its meal.

GALAPAGOS GIANT TORTOISE

The largest tortoises are found on the Galapagos Islands, off the coast of Ecuador in the Pacific Ocean. These lumbering giants are strong enough to carry a person. Each island in the Galapagos group has a variety or subspecies of giant tortoise that is recognizable by the shape of its shell or the size and length of its legs. These slight variations were noticed by English naturalist Charles Darwin when he visited the islands in the 1830s. The tortoises, finches and other animals of the Galapagos set Darwin thinking about the idea of evolution by natural selection. He described this idea in his book *On the Origin of Species* (1859), which is now central to the study of the natural world.

⬇ Several kinds of giant tortoises live on Pacific and Indian Ocean islands, such as the Galapagos.

CIRCULAR SHELL

The spiny softshell turtle has an almost circular shell, covered with leathery skin and small, spiny projections on the front. This turtle is a good swimmer and spends most of its life in water, catching insects, crustaceans and fish.

The largest freshwater turtle in North America is the alligator snapping turtle. It has a large head and a rough, lumpy shell. Inside its gaping mouth is a small, pink, fleshy flap that resembles a worm. When a fish comes to eat the "worm", it is quickly snapped up in the turtle's jaws.

⬆ The leopard tortoise of Africa has a high-domed shell with bold markings. It lives in woods and grassland.

> **BIGGEST... !**
> The largest land tortoise is the Galapagos giant tortoise. It weighs a staggering 230 kg or more and its shell can be 1.2 m long.

MAIN GROUPS OF TURTLES (continued from page 73):

Snake-necked turtles (*Chelidae*)
• about 30 species
• live mainly in water
• most have long necks
• includes giant snake-neck turtle, matamata

Helmeted side-necked turtles (*Pelomedusidae*)
• about 20 species
• live mainly in water
• includes Arrau river turtle, West African mud turtle

Alligator turtles (*Chelydridae*)
• 3 species
• large head and long tail
• live in water
• includes snapping turtle, big-headed turtle

Softshell turtles (*Trionychidae*)
• about 22 species
• shell covered with leathery skin
• live mainly in water
• includes spiny softshell, Indian flapshell

American mud and musk turtles (*Kinosternidae*)
• about 20 species
• musk glands below carapace give off strong-smelling scent
• live mainly in water
• includes striped mud turtle, common musk turtle

Pond turtles (*Emydidae*)
• about 85 species
• well-developed shell, strong limbs and webbed feet
• live mainly in water, some stay on land
• includes box turtle, river terrapin, wood turtle

Tortoises (*Testudinae*)
• about 41 species
• domed shell, strong back legs
• land-living
• includes gopher tortoise, pancake tortoise, spur-thighed tortoise, Galapagos giant tortoise

CROCODILES AND ALLIGATORS

CROCODILES HAVE CHANGED LITTLE SINCE THEY SHARED THE PREHISTORIC WORLD WITH THEIR CLOSE REPTILE RELATIVES, THE DINOSAURS, MORE THAN 100 MILLION YEARS AGO. There are three sub-groups in the crocodile group, known as crocodilians. These are the crocodiles themselves, the alligators and caimans, and the single species of gharial (gavial) from northern India. Crocodilians are found in all tropical and subtropical regions of the world. They are powerful predators, equally at home on land and in water.

🔺 The Nile crocodile has become very rare. Its natural river and swamp habitats have been drained and changed to farmland, industrial sites and tourist areas.

A typical crocodile or alligator has a long body covered with thick scales. Bony plates that are embedded in the skin along the back give further protection. The snout is long too, with nostrils and eyes set high on the head. The tail is also long and tall, and very muscular, for swimming. The two pairs of legs are short but strong, with five toes on the front feet and four on the back feet. All of these toes are partly webbed.

🔺 The massive saltwater or estuarine crocodile is regularly seen swimming offshore.

It waits for an animal to come and drink. When the prey is almost within reach, the crocodile makes a sudden dash from the water, drags the victim below the surface, and holds it there, usually with the croc's jaws clamped onto its throat, until it dies.

🔺 A crocodile is almost entirely covered in thick, horny scales, with extra plates of bone along the back.

LAZY DAYS, BUSY NIGHTS

Crocodiles spend much of the day basking in the sun on sandy riverbanks and mudflats. They become active in the evening and usually hunt for prey at night. They are among the most patient, silent, and stealthy of all large predators. Often the croc lurks in water near the shore, almost totally submerged like an old floating log.

CROC OR ALLIGATOR?

The main difference between a crocodile and an alligator is that, in an alligator, the fourth tooth on each side of the lower jaw fits into a pit in the upper jaw.

◪ The gharial's very long, narrow jaws, armed with about 100 teeth, can be swished sideways through the water at speed to grab prey. The lump or "pot" at the upper end of the snout is a feature of old males.

NEW TEETH

A crocodile has teeth which are strong and pointed, but not especially large. Each tooth is set in its own deep socket in the jawbone. As teeth become worn, they are replaced by new teeth which grow at the bases of the old ones.

ON THE MOVE

On land, crocodiles walk slowly with the legs splayed out to the sides, swinging the body with a snake-like wriggling motion. But a crocodile in a hurry holds its legs straighter, stiffer and more upright under its body. This "high walk" allows a speed of about 5 km/h. A few species, such as Johnston's crocodile, can even break into a gallop and sprint almost as fast as a person, at a speed of about 20 km/h.

In water, the crocodile is an excellent swimmer. It pushes itself along with side-to-side sweeps of its powerful tail. It can also use its tail to drive itself suddenly and powerfully out of the water, in a sudden upward lunge to snatch prey. The legs are held close against the body to reduce resistance as the reptile swishes along.

> **LARGEST... !**
>
> The biggest reptile is the saltwater or estuarine crocodile of the Indian and Pacific Oceans. It grows to 7 m long and weighs about a ton.

The tooth cannot be seen when the mouth is closed. In a crocodile, these fourth lower teeth are visible when the mouth is shut, on the outsides of the upper jaw. Crocodiles live in tropical and subtropical areas of Central and South America, Africa, Asia and Australia. Most alligators and caimans live in North, Central and South America, with one species, the Chinese alligator, in East Asia. The gharial lives in northern India and neighbouring countries, and is recognized by its very long, narrow snout.

CROCODILE DIET

The food of a crocodile or alligator tends to change as the animal grows. A young Nile crocodile less than 50 cm long feeds mostly on small creatures such as frogs, insects and spiders. As it nears 100 cm in length, it starts to catch larger prey such as birds, lizards, small mammals and fish. The full-grown Nile crocodile preys mainly on mammals up to the size of zebras.

◪ The black caiman is not always black. It may be brown and have creamy patches on its chin and underside.

◪ All crocodilians have their nostrils, eyes and ears on the top of the head. They can breathe, see and hear while almost submerged.

MAIN GROUPS OF CROCODILIANS
(continued from page 73):

Alligators and caimans
(*Alligatorinae*)
• 7 species
• teeth not visible when mouth is closed

Crocodiles (*Crocodylinae*)
• 14 species
• fourth tooth in lower jaw visible when mouth is closed
• includes mugger, false gharial

Gharial (*Gavialinae*)
• 1 species
• long, slender jaws

IGUANAS, AGAMIDS AND CHAMELEONS

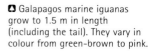

LIZARDS ARE THE LARGEST GROUP OF REPTILES. There are more than 3,700 species. They are most common in tropical areas, but there are species in nearly all regions except the far north and Antarctica. The iguanas are one of the largest lizard sub-groups. Most live in North and South America, but there are some in Madagascar and Fiji. The agamids, or chisel-teeth lizards, are similar in appearance and habits to the iguanas, but live in the Old World – Africa (except Madagascar), Asia and Australia, with one species in Europe. Most chameleons come from tropical Africa and India, and are well adapted for life in the trees.

🔺 Galapagos marine iguanas grow to 1.5 m in length (including the tail). They vary in colour from green-brown to pink.

🔺 A frilled lizard in defensive posture.

Some iguanas and agamids are quite large for lizards, growing to more than 50 cm in length (including the tail). Many are adorned with crests and frills, and the males especially are brightly coloured. They live on land and in trees, and are active during the day.

Most prey on insects and other small creatures, but a few species, such as the chuckwalla and desert iguana of North America, feed on plant material.

RUNNING AT SPEED
The basilisk lizard is a type of iguana from South America. It has very muscular back legs and long, thin toes. It is one of the fastest runners of all lizards, reaching more than 10 km/h.

🔺 Striped agama

LITTLE AND LARGE... !
Chameleons range in size from the tiny brown brookesia, about as long as a little finger, to the huge oustaleti chameleon at 55 cm long.

The basilisk lizard runs so fast that it can even move for short distances over water, its long toes supported by the skin-like film on the surface.

It runs with its long tail held out behind for balance. Male basilisks have a large, bony "helmet" on the head and crests of skin along the back and tail. In females the helmets are smaller.

DIVING BELOW
Unlike other iguanas, the marine iguana (page 73) spends much of its life in the seas around the Galapagos Islands. An expert swimmer and diver, it uses its strong tail to propel itself through water, diving to eat seaweeds. Although the iguana must come to the surface to breathe, it can eat while submerged. Its heart rate slows as it dives, to reduce its need for oxygen, so it can stay under water for longer.

FRILLED LIZARD
The frilled lizard is an agamid from Australia and New Guinea. It has a very long tail and an unusual, brightly coloured collar of skin, like a ruff, around its neck. Normally this neck frill lies folded flat against the shoulders. If the lizard is alarmed, it opens its mouth wide and spreads out the frill around its head. This makes it appear much larger, to deter possible enemies.

FLYING LIZARDS
The flying dragon is another type of agamid lizard, found in Southeast Asia. It lives in thick rainforest and has also taken to rubber tree plantations. It does not really fly, but can glide long distances between trees without having to come down to the ground. It has wing-like flaps of skin at each side of its

Chameleons change colour to blend in with their surroundings.

body, which viewed from above, make a circular shape. The flaps are held against the body, and extended as the lizard launches itself into the air.

LIFE IN THE TREES
The chameleon is adapted for hunting insects in trees. Its feet are specially arranged to provide a strong grip on branches, with three toes wrapped around one side and two on the other. The chameleon also has a strong prehensile tail, which can be curled around the branch and used like an extra leg. With these gripping aids, the chameleon can remain still for long periods. It also changes its colour to match the background. When prey comes near, the chameleon takes aim with the help of its excellent eyesight, and shoots out its long, sticky-tipped tongue at the victim.

◄ Collared lizard

SOME GROUPS OF LIZARDS:

Iguanas *(Iguanidae)*
- more than 850 species
- limbs usually well developed
- includes marine iguana, basilisk lizard, anole

Agamid lizards *(Agamidae)*
- about 350 species

- large head and long tail
- includes frilled lizard, flying dragon

Chameleons *(Chamaeleontidae)*
- 135 species
- flattened body, prehensile tail
- large eyes can move separately
- changes colour to match scenery

◄ The chameleon's tongue darts out so fast that it can reach its prey in less than one-hundredth of a second.

PYTHONS, BOAS AND THREAD SNAKES

SNAKES HAVE NO LEGS. Yet they can wriggle at speed along the ground, climb trees easily, swim well – and a few can even "fly"! Snakes are a hugely successful group of reptiles with almost 2,400 species. They live on all continents except Antarctica. They are also absent from Ireland, Iceland and New Zealand. They are all predators. Most can open their mouths wide to swallow prey whole. Some have suffocating coils and others strike with deadly poison fangs.

Snakes evolved millions of years ago, from reptiles similar to lizards which had four limbs. Gradually the limbs became smaller, and in most snakes today, they have completely disappeared. But some snakes have tiny, useless remnants of limbs, such as hip and rear leg bones. These include thread snakes, blind snakes and pipe snakes. They are called primitive snakes because they most resemble their distant ancestors. Like the first snakes, most of them burrow into soil and spend much of their lives underground.

◘ The sunbeam snake of Southeast Asia burrows and swims well, and eats fish, frogs, mice and small birds. Its body has a mixture of primitive (ancient) and advanced (modern) features.

Blind and thread snakes have tiny eyes hidden beneath scales. Most thread snakes are blunt-headed, while blind snakes have narrow heads. Both designs help them to tunnel through soil. They eat small worms, grubs, ants, termites and similar soil creatures.

PIPE SNAKES
Pipe snakes also spend much time burrowing underground. Unlike most other snakes, a pipe snake cannot open its mouth very wide. So it feeds mainly on slender-bodied animals such as worm lizards and other snakes, which it sucks in like spaghetti.

◘ The green python coils around itself to rest, almost as it would squeeze or constrict its prey.

◘ Boas often rest in trees. Like pythons, they can tilt forward the large scales on the underside of the body. This raises the rear edges of the scales for extra grip as the snake moves forwards.

Pythons are mainly large snakes of the tropics in Africa, Asia and Australia. They like to stay near water and climb trees well. Boas are similar snakes of the Americas, although they stay more on the ground. Both pythons and boas are primitive snakes, with tiny hip and back leg bones embedded in their bodies. They all have two lungs as well. Most other snakes have lost one lung during evolution, to help achieve their narrow, streamlined shape.

◁ The false coral snake is a type of pipe snake. It grows to about 80 cm long.

Both pythons and boas are fierce predators. They kill their prey by coiling their bodies around it and crushing it until the victim suffocates. They prey mainly on mammals and birds. The reticulated python is the longest snake, reaching 10 m. Boas have slightly different bones in the head and the teeth compared to pythons. They include the second-longest but heaviest snake, the anaconda. The anaconda spends much of its life in swamps and slow-moving streams, in its rainforest habitat. Half-hidden in the shallows, it lies in wait for animals to come and drink. When a victim is near enough, the anaconda bites and envelops it in crushing coils.

HEAVIEST... !

The bulkiest snake is the anaconda, a type of boa. It weighs up to 250 kg, which is more than three adult humans.

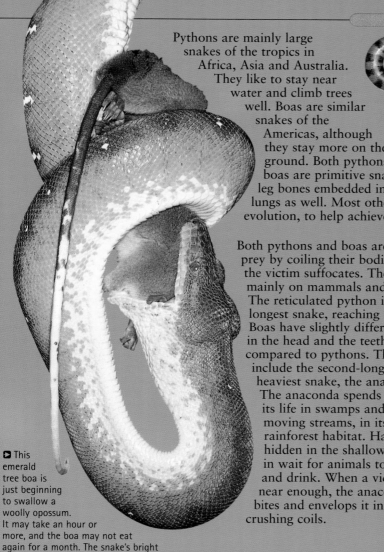

▷ This emerald tree boa is just beginning to swallow a woolly opossum. It may take an hour or more, and the boa may not eat again for a month. The snake's bright green body gives excellent camouflage among the leaves of its forest home in northern South America.

◭ The western blind snake is a type of thread snake. It has very small, simple eyes hidden beneath its skin. It can slide into ants' nests to eat the larvae.

CARING MOTHER
Most snakes lay their eggs in holes and leave them to hatch. The Indian python is one of the few snake species that incubate their eggs with their own bodies. The female lays up to 100 eggs and curls around them to keep them warm and protected. She also adjusts her body to cover them more or less, according to the weather.

🌐 World Watch

Large snakes such as pythons and boas were once hunted for their leathery, beautifully patterned skin. This was used to make shoes, bags, belts, trousers and similar hard-wearing items. However, the hunting made some species extremely rare. It is more difficult to farm snakes for the skin trade compared to, for example, crocodiles. Most snakes will only eat a victim if it has only just died and is still warm.

◭ The anaconda is a massive-bodied swamp snake from South America. It grows to 9 m in length and can eat animals the size of goats, tapirs and peccaries. Females give birth to about 30 babies, each 60 cm long.

SOME GROUPS OF SNAKES
(continued from page 73):

Thread snakes
(Leptotyphlopidae)
• about 64 species
• small, slender body, blunt head and tail

Blind snakes (Typhlopidae)
• about 150 species
• smooth, cylindrical body
• teeth only in upper jaw

Pipe snakes (Aniliidae)
• 11 species
• blunt head
• body often boldly marked
• includes coral pipe snake, false coral snake

Pythons and boas (Boidae)
• about 60 species
• flexible jaws
• tiny remnants of rear limbs
• squeeze or constrict prey

81

☑ The white pelican is one of the biggest waterbirds, with a wingspan of 2.7 m. It is known for its big beak with a stretchy pouch.

SECTION 6
BIRDS

BIRDS ARE PROBABLY THE MOST EASILY RECOGNIZED OF ALL ANIMALS. Any creature with wings, feathers and a beak must be a bird. But not all birds use their wings for flying. The ostrich uses its wings as a sunshade to keep its eggs cool in the desert heat. Puffins, razorbills and guillemots flap their wings to swim underwater, with the help of their webbed feet.

Feathers and beaks vary enormously, too. The kiwi is flightless, like the ostrich, and its feathers look like hairs. The peacock's colourful tail feathers are longer than your arm. The shape of a bird's beak usually shows the type of food it eats. An eagle's beak is sharp and hooked, for tearing flesh. A parrot's beak is thick and massive, for cracking nuts. A pelican's beak has a stretchy throat pouch which it uses as a fishing bag. A curlew's beak is like long, slim tweezers for probing into mud.

Birds are one of only two groups of animals that are warm-blooded. (The other group is mammals.) Being warm-blooded means being able to stay active even in cold conditions. Penguins survive some of the lowest temperatures on Earth, in the bitter cold and driving snow of Antarctica. Other birds experience intense cold at great heights, on mountains and during long-distance journeys. Some migrating geese fly as high as jet planes.

FLIGHTLESS BIRDS

■ The dodo was a huge-beaked, turkey-sized flightless bird from the Indian Ocean island of Mauritius. In this remote place it had no natural predators and so no need to fly. But when European people came to the island in the 1500s, they brought rats, pigs and monkeys, which ate the dodos' eggs. By 1680, they were extinct – "dead as a dodo".

ALL BIRDS HAVE WINGS, BUT NOT ALL OF THEM CAN FLY. Penguins are so well adapted to life in the sea that they use their short, stubby wings for swimming, not flying. The rare kakapo parrot of New Zealand has lost the power of flight because it has no natural predators where it lives, and so does not need to escape by flying. The most distinctive flightless birds are the ratites. These are mostly big – ostriches, emus, cassowaries, rheas and kiwis. They are part of a group of birds that, like penguins, never evolved the ability to fly. Ratites have always walked or run everywhere.

■ The emu of Australia grows up to 170 cm tall and weighs almost 45 kg. In some areas they have become pests because they eat crops and break fences.

OUCH! ⚠

The kiwi's huge white eggs are the biggest eggs of any bird, compared to the size of the adult. Each egg weighs about 454 g, which is almost a quarter of the mother's normal body weight – and she may lay two of them!

FLYING IN WATER

Penguins are so well adapted to life in the water that their wings are more like flippers. Their coats are so thick and well waterproofed with oil that they can survive even in the icy waters of the Antarctic. They are superb swimmers, and dash through the water by flapping their wings with the same motion that other birds use to fly through the air. On snow and ice, penguins often slide head-first down slopes, as if tobogganing. In the water they are swift and agile, pursuing their prey with ease. They eat mainly krill, squid and fish. Emperor penguins are the largest species. They can dive as deep as 250 m in search of food.

BIGGEST BIRDS

Millions of years ago there were many species of ratites all over the world. Now there are just ten species left, scattered as far apart as Africa and New Zealand. They are different to other birds in various ways, besides being flightless. For example, their feathers lack the smooth, flat, airproof surfaces which other birds have for flying. Instead, ratites have downy, "hairy" feathers. The leg bones of ratites are sturdy, more like a mammal's legs than a bird's. This is why some ratites can grow so large. The ostrich is the biggest living bird, towering up to 2.75 m tall.

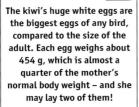

◀ Penguins dive into the water in a large group to hunt for their food. The mass dive helps to confuse any predators such as leopard seals and killer whales that may be lurking nearby.

◀ The world's biggest bird, the ostrich, is also the only bird with just two toes on each foot. The toes have sharp claws, and a kick from an ostrich can be deadly.

Even bigger than an ostrich was the giant moa of New Zealand. Some moas were 3 m tall and weighed as much as a pony. They became extinct after people arrived.

OSTRICHES AND RHEAS

With their soft, downy plumage and bare necks, ostriches look rather comical and vulnerable as they strut across the grasslands of Africa. But they can sprint at up to 60 km/h, and can kick like a mule – which is why they rarely fall prey to lions. The idea that they bury their heads in the sand when afraid is a myth. It comes from the way the bird moves its eggs in the nest so that they stay evenly warm.

The cassowary uses its helmet-like head crest for pushing through thick scrub.

The rhea lives on the plains of southern Brazil and Argentina. It looks like a small ostrich, but has more feathers on its neck, and larger wings. On rare occasions it can struggle a very short distance through the air. Unusually for birds, male rheas and ostriches do most of the work at breeding time. The male scoops out a hole in the ground for a nest. Then, when several females have laid their eggs in it, he keeps them safe and at the correct temperature until they hatch, and he cares for the young chicks too.

The flightless kakapo of New Zealand is the world's largest parrot. It was once thought to have been wiped out by cats, rats and dogs. But recently, a few survivors were found and taken to a protected area on Little Barrier Island near Auckland, where there are no such predators. There the kakapos can breed and the species might be saved.

AUSTRALIAN RATITES

In the thick forests of tropical Australia and nearby islands, such as New Guinea, live three species of shy ratites called cassowaries. They are the same size as rheas, about 1.5 m tall. But they look more like long-legged turkeys, with a brightly coloured neck and a bony crest. They eat fruits, seeds and other plant parts. Another Australian ratite is the emu. It is second only to the ostrich in size, and can run almost as fast. It eats an extremely varied diet in grasslands and woodlands.

New Zealand's ratites are chicken-sized kiwis. Their wings are tiny, hidden beneath fur-like feathers. Kiwis are secretive birds, active only at night in bushy scrub or forests. They are rarely seen as they search for grubs, insects, berries and fruit.

Kiwis are tubby birds, covered in shaggy feathers like a furball. They have the best sense of smell of almost any bird, using the nostrils on the end of the beak to sniff out food in the leaves and soil.

> ### LARGEST... !
> The biggest bird of historic times was the elephant bird of Madagascar. This gigantic ratite almost lived up to its name. It grew up to 4.5 m tall and weighed as much as an ox. Its eggs had a volume of 7 litres, the size of a soccer ball.

BIRDS (AVES)

- about 8,800 species
- warm-blooded
- feathers
- beak or bill

Some flightless birds:

Ostrich
- 1 species
- Africa
- savanna
- male black and white; female brown

Rheas
- 2 species
- South America
- scrub, grassland
- brown or grey

Emu
- 1 species
- Australia
- woodland, scrub, and grassland
- dark brown

Cassowaries
- 3 species
- Australia, New Guinea
- rainforest
- mainly black

Penguins
- 16 species
- Antarctic region and southern parts of main oceans

- rocky islands and icebergs
- mainly black and white
- expert swimmers

Kiwis
- 3 species
- New Zealand
- forest and scrub
- brown or grey

Tinamous
- 49 species
- Central and South America
- resemble guinea fowl or pheasants
- some can fly but do so rarely

SEABIRDS

HUGE NUMBERS OF BIRDS LIVE BY, OR ON, THE SEA. Some feed mainly along the shore or dive for fish in coastal waters, such as various gulls, cormorants and gannets. Others, like auks, terns, skuas and frigate birds, live for weeks far out in the ocean. They come to the surface occasionally in calm weather, to float and rest. Still others, such as albatrosses, shearwaters and petrels, spend weeks at a time in the air. They land only rarely, usually to breed. They are superb flyers, soaring across the oceans for thousands of kilometres.

🔼 Shearwater

🔼 Albatrosses may be at sea for 2–3 weeks at a time. The wandering albatross has the longest wingspan of any bird, at up to 3.5 m. The waved albatross shown here is slightly smaller.

🔽 The male frigatebird has a bright red, balloon-like skin pouch on his throat. He blows this up to attract a female.

There are about 90 species of gulls, skuas and terns. They usually wheel and call along the coast, but gulls especially have adapted to new sources of food far inland. They hunt for worms and grubs in freshly ploughed fields, and squabble over leftovers on rubbish tips, especially in winter. The herring gull, in particular, is aggressive and threatens other birds. Gulls eat almost anything, including fish, crabs, insects, rotten meat and the eggs of other birds.

Most gulls have white and grey plumage, matching the reflections of sunlight on the sea. Some species have black markings on the back, wings and head. The larger gulls, like the great black-backed gull, have heavy, hooked beaks. They can easily kill smaller birds, baby rabbits and similar prey.

🔼 Boobies were named from the Spanish word *bobo*, meaning "stupid", because these birds were easily caught by sailors for food.

🔽 Guillemot

PIRATES AMONG BIRDS

Skuas resemble the larger gulls and have fearsome hooked beaks. In North America they are known by the German name of jaeger, meaning "hunter", due to their habit of chasing other birds who are carrying food. They harass the other bird, force it to drop its meal, then swoop to steal it. Big skuas like the great skua may catch and kill birds even larger than themselves.

Terns are like slim, graceful gulls. Many have forked tails, earning them the nickname of "sea-swallows". Many terns catch their fish prey by plunge-diving straight down into the water.

◀ Royal terns

◀ Common gulls use the wind to stay aloft without flapping.

They are mainly summer visitors to temperate regions, migrating to warmer areas to avoid the cold winter months.

SKIMMING ALONG

Skimmers are tern-like birds, but with an unusual feature. The lower mandible (part of the beak) is longer than the upper part. The skimmer flies low and dips this lower mandible in the water, to snatch any fish.

MASTERS OF THE OCEAN WINDS

Albatrosses and petrels are master flyers, feeding far out at sea. Albatrosses are so big and heavy that they usually need a cliff to leap from, or a headwind to launch themselves into the air. Once aloft, they glide for hours in winds and air currents, without flapping. Shearwaters are smaller but have similar bodies, with long, narrow wings. Storm petrels are smaller and darker.

PLUMP DIVERS

Auks are plump seabirds resembling penguins. Their tight feathering keeps body warmth in and water out. They spend much time diving for food. Guillemots and razorbills breed in colonies on rocky ledges and cliffs, where most predators cannot reach.

Cormorants are related to pelicans and have a similar but smaller throat pouch. Their feet are webbed across all four toes. They are black or dark birds, expert at diving and swimming after fish. They prefer rocky coasts and, unusually for seabirds, the oily waterproofing on their feathers is not very effective. So they spend long periods sitting with their wings spread out to dry in the sun.

FRIGATEBIRDS

Frigatebirds live along tropical coasts and are among the most graceful seabirds. The magnificent frigatebird has long wings and a long tail, which it uses as an aerial rudder and air-brake. It can swoop to catch fish leaping above the surface or snatch baby turtles hatching from their eggs on the beach.

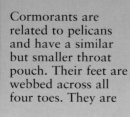

◀ The puffin is a strange-looking seabird that nests in clifftop burrows. Its brightly patterned beak is large enough to hold a dozen small fish such as sand-eels.

SOME GROUPS OF SEABIRDS:	
Gulls and terns • 95 species • mostly white or grey • narrow wings	• black and white plumage
Skuas (jaegers) • 6 species • brown and white • hooked beak	**Cormorants** • 29 species • black or dark plumage • swim low in water
Skimmers • 3 species • black or dark brown and white • long lower bill	**Gannets and boobies** • 9 species • white, with black or dark markings
Albatrosses, shearwaters, and petrels • 93 species • oceanic • long, narrow wings	**Frigate birds** • 5 species • large and long-winged • black or dark and white
Auks • 22 species • compact and dumpy • dive well	**Tropicbirds** • 3 species • white with black markings • graceful flyers • tail streamers

HERONS, DUCKS AND GEESE

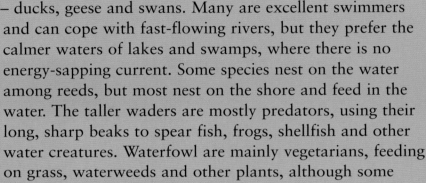

🔺 At more than 3 m, the marabou stork of Africa has the largest wingspan of any land bird.

THE FRESH WATERS OF LAKES, RIVERS AND MARSHES ARE HOME TO A WEALTH OF BIRDS. There are long-legged waders like herons, storks and flamingoes, smaller cranes and rails, and hundreds of species of waterfowl – ducks, geese and swans. Many are excellent swimmers and can cope with fast-flowing rivers, but they prefer the calmer waters of lakes and swamps, where there is no energy-sapping current. Some species nest on the water among reeds, but most nest on the shore and feed in the water. The taller waders are mostly predators, using their long, sharp beaks to spear fish, frogs, shellfish and other water creatures. Waterfowl are mainly vegetarians, feeding on grass, waterweeds and other plants, although some ducks take insects and shellfish.

🔺 The mute swan weighs 18 kg. It needs a long stretch of water for take-off and landing.

🔻 Flamingoes live and nest in huge colonies in the tropics. To feed, a flamingo bends its neck and tips its head over, to hold its strange, kinked beak upside-down and sweep it from side to side. Inside the beak, the tongue works like a piston to suck water in and squirt it out. Hair-like fringes on the beak filter out small shrimps and similar food.

Most wading birds have long, featherless legs for striding through the water, a long neck to reach down and feed, and a long beak to grab or stab prey. The biggest group of large freshwater waders includes herons, egrets and bitterns, with 60 species throughout temperate and tropical regions. Most are grey or brown. When hunting fish and frogs, a heron stands motionless on one leg in the shallows, apparently asleep, until it suddenly spears down into the water with its long beak. The prey is caught and then flipped around so the bird can swallow it head-first.

Herons fly slowly with extravagant, steady wingbeats. They keep their long necks tucked into their shoulders – unlike cranes, storks and ibises, which fly, with the head and neck extended. Herons usually nest in colonies called heronries, building their untidy pile-of-sticks nests high in trees.

SOARING STORKS

Storks are even bigger than herons, some standing 1.2 m tall. They fly through the air with slow, strong wingbeats, neck stretched out in front and legs trailing behind. On their long annual journeys, or migrations, they find an up-current of warm air to gain height, then flap on their way.

In Europe and Asia, white storks often build their great twig nests on the roofs of houses. Many people see the return of the same pair year after year from Africa, to build their nest in the same place, as a sign of continuing good luck. Storks raise their young with great care.

BOOM BOOM!

The male bittern has one of the loudest bird calls. It is an extraordinary boom, made to warn others off its territory. The bittern makes this deep booming in its throat, and it can sound almost like a bull roaring as it echoes across the marsh at night. The bittern's scientific name is <u>Botaurus</u>, which comes from an ancient Latin term meaning "bellow of the bull".

SPOON-FED

Spoonbills are medium-sized waders named after their flattened, spoon-shaped beaks. The spoonbill swishes its beak from side to side through the water, to catch prey such as fish and small crabs.

Spoonbills are close relatives of ibises. An ibis has a long, thin, down-curved beak. Like spoonbills, ibises have webbed toes to help them swim and walk on soft mud. Both ibises

and spoonbills feed in muddy water, detecting prey with their sensitive beaks. The brilliant pink plumage of the scarlet ibis makes it one of the most striking of all tropical birds.

◣ Scarlet ibis

WATERFOWL

The body of a duck or goose is so buoyant, it can float for hours, paddling with its big webbed feet. But on land, waterfowl – especially ducks – waddle awkwardly. The pochard and tufted duck are diving ducks, descending to the bottom to find roots, shoots, shellfish and insects. Dabbling ducks such as the mallard lap at the water's surface, or up-end to sift waterweeds and snails from the muddy bed.

Swans are the largest waterfowl. A swan uses its long, elegant neck to reach down and grab plant bits and small creatures. Most swans have pure white plumage, apart from the black swan of Australia and the black-neck swan of South America. Geese are slightly smaller, and come onto land to graze on grass. Geese and ducks are powerful long-distance flyers. Bar-headed geese have been seen from planes at altitudes of 9,000 m crossing the Himalayas. Many geese breed in the Arctic and migrate south in the autumn to warmer places.

◣ The heron is a patient hunter, standing still and silent on one leg for hours. Then it makes a lightning dart with its long beak, to spear a fish which mistook the heron's single leg for a reed stem.

▶ The roseate spoonbill is one of the most colourful of waders. It dwells in the warmer areas of the Americas.

HERONS, EGRETS AND BITTERNS		
• 60 species • long legs, long neck, long bill • most species are quite large • neck curved or hunched back in flight	• neck outstretched in flight Flamingoes • 4 species • long legs, long neck, stubby bill • large, with pink plumage • neck outstretched in flight	• most species are long-necked • bill usually flattened, quite short and wide (spatulate) Some groups of ducks, geese and swans: Swans and geese
Storks • 17 species • long legs, long neck, long bill • most species are quite large • neck outstretched in flight	Cranes • 15 species • tall, with long legs and neck • white or grey • neck outstretched in flight	• 21 species Dabbling ducks • 40 species Sea ducks • 20 species Diving ducks • 16 species Shelducks • 16 species Perching ducks • 13 species Whistling ducks • 9 species Stifftails • 8 species
Spoonbills and ibises • 31 species • long legs, long neck, bill curved or flattened	Ducks, geese, swans • 150 species • webbed feet, good swimmers	

BIRDS OF PREY

A SHARP, HOOKED BEAK AND CURVED CLAWS CALLED TALONS MARK OUT THE RAPTORS – BIRDS OF PREY – AS THE DEADLY HUNTERS OF THE BIRD WORLD. Most are masterful flyers, able to stay aloft for hours while searching for prey with their incredibly keen eyes. Then they dive like a bullet onto the chosen victim. Smaller raptors like the sharp-shinned hawk are no bigger than a robin. They eat mainly insects, frogs and similar small creatures. Hawks and eagles take rats and rabbits, snakes and lizards, and other birds. The huge harpy eagle of the Amazon jungle snatches monkeys and sloths from the treetops. The osprey and fish eagles grab fish. Vultures and condors feed mostly on carrion (dead animals).

◖ Despite wildlife protection laws, golden eagles are still shot and poisoned by farmers and gamekeepers.

◖ The hobby is one of the most brightly coloured of hawks. It is so speedy and agile that it can catch dragonflies, swallows and swifts.

There are some 295 species of raptors. They hunt across a huge range of habitats, from mountains to rainforests. The condors are among the largest flying birds, with wingspans of 3 m. Falcons such as the peregrine are the greatest winged acrobats, able to catch other birds in mid-flight with amazing agility.

All kinds of large predators, such as sharks and tigers, are scarce because of the balance of nature. This also applies to large birds of prey, especially eagles. Sadly, people try to kill them in case they attack farm animals or gamebirds. And they are shot as trophies, or their eggs are stolen for collectors.

◖ The gyrfalcon is a powerful flyer. It plunges, or stoops, from above at tremendous speed, to grip its victim in its sharp-taloned feet. Hawks do this too, but they kill their prey with their claws, whereas a falcon's fatal blow is a sharp bite to the neck.

DIVE! ⚠

The peregrine falcon is the fastest-moving of all animals. It can streak down onto prey, or charge at an intruder in its territory, in a powered dive called a stoop. Some stoops have been timed at more than 350 km/h.

◪ A buzzard glides on a warm air current, waiting to spot its prey.

They soar high and scan the scene below, ready to swoop. The kestrel is often known as the windhover, because it hovers in mid-air, wings and tail moving but head held still, focusing on the ground. When it sees a victim, it drops suddenly and pounces on its prey.

◪ The bald eagle is not bald, but its white head looks featherless from a distance. It is a fish-eater, like the osprey.

Many large raptors survive today only in remote, often mountainous terrain. However others, like certain kestrels and kites, have adapted to living near people. They wheel over high-rise city buildings and motorways, just as they would soar along cliffs or shores.

SYMBOL OF POWER

Eagles, with their graceful soaring that can turn into a deadly swoop, have long been symbols of power. The bald eagle is the national bird of the USA. The golden eagle was the figurehead of the armies of Ancient Rome. The golden eagle is often called the "king of birds". It hunts rabbits, marmots, ground squirrels and birds. Its nest, or "eyrie", is a bed of twigs perched high on a cliff, to which pairs return year after year.

The American bald eagle has been the victim of hunting, water pollution and loss of natural habitat. By the mid-1970s there were just 2,000 left in the USA. Conservation laws were introduced and now there are more than 20,000.

◪ The osprey has rough-skinned toes which help the sharp, curved claws to grip slippery fish.

WINGED SCAVENGERS

The biggest birds of prey are not predators, but carrion feeders. Vultures and condors have weak bills and the flesh they eat must be soft and rotten before they can rip off mouthfuls. The bearded vulture or lammergeier takes bones from the carcass and flies high to drop them onto rocks. The bones smash to reveal the soft, juicy marrow inside. All of the vultures have vast wings and spend hours soaring high, peering across the landscape for corpses. Condors have such keen smell that they can even locate dead meat under a canopy of trees by scent alone.

Condors are among the biggest flying birds. The wingspan of the Andean condor of South America can exceed 3 m. Sadly, as a result of human persecution, the Californian condor is now one of the world's rarest birds. It also tends to crash into power cables. Conservationists in the 1980s captured the few remaining wild birds in a desperate bid to breed them in captivity. Some of the young have been released into the wild, but this species remains on the very edge of extinction.

◪ The rare Everglades kite feeds only on one type of water snail, the apple snail.

SMALLER RAPTORS

Hawks, sparrowhawks, goshawks, falcons, kestrels and hobbies are smaller than eagles. They often take other birds as well as ground-living animals.

There are two main kinds of hawks: accipiters and buteos. Accipiters, such as the goshawk, tend to wait on a branch and then dash out to ambush smaller birds under the cover of the foliage. They have short, rounded wings and a long, narrow tail, for great manoeuvrability. Buteos, such as the kestrel, have longer wings and fan-shaped tails.

MAIN BIRDS OF PREY:	Osprey *(fish eagle)*
	• 1 species
Eagles, hawks, buzzards and	• worldwide
vultures	• hunts fish
• 224 species	• brown and white
• worldwide	
• medium to large	Falcons, falconets and caracaras
• sharp hooked beak	• 62 species
• sharp curved talons	• worldwide
	• small to medium
American vultures	• long tail
• 7 species	
• large	Secretary bird
• naked head and neck	• 1 species
• soaring flight	• African grassland
	• long legs and feathered head crest
	• eats reptiles

PIGEONS, DOVES AND PARROTS

CITY PIGEONS MAY NOT BE THE MOST APPEALING BIRDS, DRAB AND GREY, LEAVING A MESS AS THEY FLOCK AROUND LITTER.

❶ Parrots have strong hooked beaks to crack open nuts and scoop out soft fruits.

❶ Crowned pigeon

Parrots, on the other hand, are among the most attractive of birds, with their vivid colours of scarlet, emerald and turquoise, their beady eyes, and their ability to mimic our voices and "talk". But pigeons and parrots have several features in common. Both eat mainly seeds and fruits. Both are bold and curious, but also placid and easy-going. And both have long associations with people. Parrots and doves live near or even in our villages, towns and cities. Many kinds, including the small members of the parrot group called parakeets, are kept as cage birds and pets. Pigeons and doves are entered for shows and competitions such as racing, and they are even used for carrying messages because of their amazing homing instincts.

Besides familiar town pigeons, there are nearly 300 other pigeon species around the world, ranging from the large and spectacular crowned pigeons of New Guinea to tiny ground doves. In general, the larger and plumper types are called pigeons and the smaller, slimmer species are known as doves. All are

❷ The budgerigar is a small species of parrot from Australia. It is mainly green for camouflage. Flocks of budgies swoop and chatter around waterholes at dusk.

mainly seed-eaters, and most build untidy stick nests in trees. Pigeons are also among the strongest-flying birds, and many migrate long distances. Most pigeons and doves have soothing, rather sad-sounding, cooing songs. These can often be heard in woods, parks and gardens, especially in early morning and evening.

◧ The pigeons in our cities are not truly wild, but part-wild or feral. This means they are descended from domestic pigeons, which were kept widely in the past, both to carry messages and to eat! Those domestic pigeons, in turn, were descended from wild rock doves, whose natural habitats are sea cliffs and rocky crags.

◖ Lorikeets like the Australian varied lorikeet, have long beaks to reach nectar in flowers.

Pigeons and doves are the only birds that feed their young on "milk", like mammals. The parent produces a milky substance from the lining of its throat, to feed to the chicks.

PARROTS
Parrots are tropical birds with strong hooked beaks and bright plumage. They also have clinging feet, with two toes pointing forwards and two backwards. This design allows a parrot to clamber in trees, using its beak as a "third foot". The real foot can also hold fruits and nuts, to eat.

There are more than 300 species in the parrot group, including macaws, lories, lorikeets, cockatoos, lovebirds and parakeets. Many are inquisitive and investigate objects with great care, holding and pecking them to see if they are good to eat. Many of the larger species are also long-lived, surviving for 30, 40 or more years in captivity. These are further reasons why they are so popular as cage birds and even as pet "companions". Sadly, this popularity means thousands of parrots are illegally captured from the wild each year. And perhaps half suffer and die before they reach the pet shops. Several kinds of parrot are now endangered in the wild as a result of this cruel and unlawful trade.

BRUSH-TIPPED TONGUES
Lories and lorikeets are colourful parrots from Southeast Asia and Australia. Unlike most other parrots they feed not on seeds and fruits, but on pollen and nectar from flowers. They have brush-like tips on their tongues to lick up these foods.

CRESTED COCKATOOS
The cockatoos have feathered crests on their heads, which they fan out when excited, such as when a predator or rival approaches.

Some species are white or pinkish. Largest is the palm cockatoo of New Guinea and northeast Australia.

THE REAL MACAW
Macaws are big, long-tailed parrots that live in the forests of Central and South America. They rest and nest in tree trunk holes. They are colourful even by parrot standards, in shades of brilliant blue, red, yellow and green.

◖ The crested cockatoo only erects its crest when aroused in some way.

Most parrots have few natural enemies, apart from hawks and eagles, and monkeys who may steal eggs and chicks. But continuing threats from the pet trade mean many are still endangered.

Parrots, cockatoos and lories	Pigeons and doves
• 330 species	• 300 species
• strong hooked beak	• dumpy bodies
• two toes face forwards, two backwards	• tree-dwelling
• bright greens or reds	• mournful calls
• mainly tropical or southern hemisphere	

◖ The gold-and-blue macaw has a beak so strong that it can easily crack open Brazil nuts.

OWLS AND NIGHTJARS

MOST HUNTING BIRDS FLY BY DAY, BUT OWLS, NIGHTJARS AND FROGMOUTHS HUNT AT NIGHT. They rely on their amazing twilight vision and even more astonishing hearing to locate their prey in the dark. Owls have enormous eyes that take up over half of the skull. They can see in almost pitch darkness. Also their ears are four times more sensitive than a cat's ears. On a quiet night an owl can hear a mouse move 45 m away. It can also pinpoint the direction of sounds with incredible accuracy. Nightjars, too, have large eyes that see especially well at twilight. They feed mainly on moths and other night-flying insects. Frogmouths are also dusk-flying birds, but they tend to swoop from a perch onto prey on the ground.

Owls live in most parts of the world, from the tropics almost to the Arctic regions. There are some 135 species. They vary in size, but all are similar in appearance with a big, broad head, no obvious neck and a saucer-shaped ruff of feathers, called the facial disc, around the huge eyes. Both eyes face directly forward, unlike those of most birds, which look partly to the side.

THE WISE OLD OWL
The owl's intense forward stare has made it a symbol of wisdom since ancient times (although owls are no more intelligent than other birds). In fact the eyes fit so tightly in the skull bone that they cannot swivel in their sockets. To look to the side, an owl twists its neck and turns its whole head. It can do this to look directly behind!

◁ The potoo (left) is a relative of the nightjar. Its name comes from its ooo-ing call. The frogmouth (below) hunts on the forest floor for beetles, snails and other small animals. It has even been known to take whole mice and small birds into its gaping mouth, which is surrounded by sensitive bristles for feeling food in the dark.

The tiny elf owl from the southern USA and Mexico is one of the smallest owls. It measures only about 12 cm from beak tip to tail tip. Largest is the European eagle owl, which can be 70 cm long, with a wingspan of 1.5 m.

◁ Most owls are mottled grey or brown. But the male snowy owl is almost pure white, the perfect disguise in its snowy Arctic habitat.

The great horned owl does not have horns. Its ear-like tufts are simply extra-long feathers. It is one of North America's largest owls, standing almost 60 cm tall.

The nightjar's song is a mechanical "churring" that resembles the sound of a distant motorcycle.

The short-eared owl is one of several owls that hunt by day as well as by night.

The oilbird of South America is a relative of the nightjars. It is unusual among the owl-like birds, in many ways. It spends all day deep in its breeding cave, then comes out at night to feed – not on insects, but on oily fruits. Oilbirds find their way in the total darkness of their cave in the way that bats do, by making loud clicking sounds and analyzing the echoes.

Owls are wonderfully adapted for night hunting. They have sharp sight and keen hearing, and their wing feathers have soft, almost furry, edges. This muffles the sound of the wings' beating and swooping, so the owl's prey is not disturbed. Smaller owls eat mostly insects. Medium-sized owls, like the barn owl and boobook (morepork), eat mice, rats, lizards and similar creatures. The biggest owls catch rabbits and squirrels. Eagle owls prey on other birds, including owls and hawks, and even carry away young deer. The fishing owls of Africa and Asia swoop on fish, frogs and crayfish, dipping just under the surface to grab prey with their sharp claws.

BIG-MOUTHED BIRDS

Nightjars glide gracefully after flying insects, which they snap up in their wide, gaping mouth. Like bats and the oilbird, they may use a type of sonar or echolocation to find their way and avoid obstacles in the dark. After the hunt, nightjars roost by day – but not hidden away in holes, caves or buildings, like owls. The nightjar rests in the open. It nestles against a tree branch or among leaves on the forest floor. This may sound risky, but its mottled plumage is such perfect camouflage that the bird is almost impossible to spot.

Frogmouths are named after their wide, gaping mouths. They are not very agile in flight. Instead, they catch their prey by dropping onto the ground from a twig or rock. Like nightjars, frogmouths rest by day in the open, relying on their camouflaged plumage for protection.

The little owl has the dished face typical of all owls. The dish shape acts as a sound trap to funnel the faintest noises towards the owl's super-sensitive ears, under the feathers on the sides of its head.

Owls	Nightjars and frogmouths
• 135 species	• 100 species
• most are nocturnal	• nocturnal
• soft feathers	• sleek and graceful
• large, flat face	• large eyes
• huge eyes	• gaping mouth
• hooked beak	• camouflaged plumage
• sharp claws	
• camouflaged plumage	

CROWS, SHRIKES AND BOWERBIRDS

MORE THAN TWO THIRDS OF BIRDS – MORE THAN 5,000 DIFFERENT SPECIES – BELONG TO THE GROUP KNOWN AS PERCHING BIRDS OR

A male blue bird of paradise shows off his plumage.

PASSERINES. Of course, many kinds of bird perch. But passerines have a special design, a four-toed foot, with three toes pointing forwards and one facing backwards. This allows them to cling securely to a twig, branch or other perch, but not to swim easily or run fast on the ground. So passerines tend to live in or near trees and bushes, where they can hop among the branches and find places to build nests. Most passerines are small. Crows, shrikes, bowerbirds and the lyrebird are among the biggest species.

White-cheeked bulbul

LARGEST... !
Ravens are the largest perching birds. These powerful members of the crow family can reach 65 cm beak-to-tail length. They can kill prey as large as a rabbit, but they usually scavenge on dead animals.

A male lyrebird courts the female from the top of an earthen mound about 90 cm across, which he builds himself.

There are more than 100 species in the crow group, including rooks, jackdaws, jays, magpies and the largest type, ravens. Most are noisy, bold, aggressive birds, which bully other bird species and are not especially afraid of other animals or even people. Jays screech and squawk all year except during the breeding season, when they go quiet so as not to give away their nests. Most crows collect and hoard bits of food and other items. European jays even "steal" shiny objects such as bottletops and rings. Most crows have black or drab plumage, except for jays such as the blue jay, and also some magpies, which are quite colourful.

A black cuckoo shrike feeds its chicks.

THE BUTCHER BIRDS
Shrikes are like birds of prey, but smaller. They lack sharp talons, but they do have a fierce-looking hooked beak, used to catch large insects, mice, lizards and frogs. A shrike usually sits in a bush or similar lookout, watching for prey. It may store surplus food by impaling the carcasses on long thorns, to eat later. This gruesome "larder" has earned the shrike the name of butcher bird.

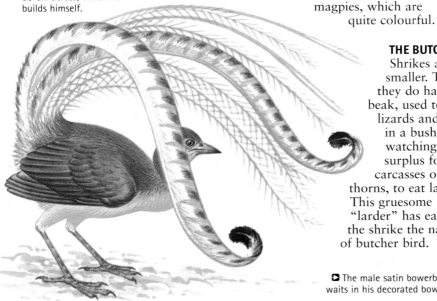

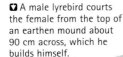
The male satin bowerbird waits in his decorated bower.

STARLINGS

Starlings are active, noisy birds that often gather together in huge flocks to feed or roost. In winter a starling roost may number thousands of birds. As dusk falls they gather somewhere such as a clump of evergreen trees or the ledges of a building. Mynahs, bulbuls and mockingbirds, which live in the Americas, are related to starlings. Mockingbirds mimic human laughter, hence their name. Their songs are loud, clear and musical.

COME INTO MY BOWER

Bowerbirds take courtship to an amazing extreme. These medium-sized birds from the forests of New Guinea and Australia build elaborate bowers. These are places where the male bird displays to his mate.

Each male decorates his bower with flowers, shells, pebbles, berries, leaves and moss. He may even use natural coloured plant juices to "paint" some of the bower's decorations.

➲ Blue jays frequent parks and gardens in eastern North America.

PARADISE

Perhaps the most spectacular of the larger passerines are the birds of paradise. They inhabit tropical forests, mainly in Southeast Asia. The males are adorned with amazing coloured plumes and perform elaborate dances to attract females during the breeding season. The male lyrebird of southeast Australia also sings and displays to attract a female. He fans out and tips forward his lyre-shaped tail streamers, while producing a rich, melodious song that includes sounds like car engines and burglar alarms!

➲ The hill mynah, from India, is sometimes kept as a cage bird for its skill in imitating noises, especially the human voice.

➲ The male Baltimore oriole sings his courtship song for a female.

➲ The male spotted bowerbird builds an elaborate courting area, or bower, of twigs and grass decorated with fruits, seeds and pebbles. The bower helps to attract a female.

SOME PERCHING BIRD GROUPS:

Bulbuls • 118 species	Mockingbirds • 30 species
Crows • 116 species	Orioles • 28 species
Starlings and mynahs • 106 species	Bowerbirds • 18 species
Birds of paradise • 43 species	Lyrebirds • 2 species
Shrikes • 70 species	

SPARROWS, FINCHES AND WEAVERS

SPARROWS, FINCHES AND WEAVER BIRDS ARE FAMILIAR IN GARDENS AND COUNTRYSIDE AROUND THE WORLD. Many species migrate from Europe to Africa in winter. Most of these birds have short, strong, stubby, pointed beaks designed for feeding on seeds. They are sometimes called seed-eating passerines (page 96). There are some 315 species in the New World (the Americas), including cardinals and buntings, and 375 in the Old World, including goldfinches, waxbills and weavers. They tend to be sociable, feeding and roosting in flocks so as to gain safety in numbers. Some kinds, especially weavers, even breed in groups or colonies. Weaver birds get their name from their nests, woven like baskets from plant stems, twigs, grass and strips of leaves.

◄ Male village weaver

◄ The male paradise whydah's tail feathers are four times as long as his body. He flies with them angled almost straight up when courting the female.

LOTS! ⚠

The red-billed quelea of Africa is one of the world's most abundant birds. It is a kind of weaver and gathers in gigantic flocks numbering a million or more birds. They wheel and turn together, darkening the sky. They also ruin crops.

Most sparrows are stocky, active birds with drab brownish plumage. Few birds are more familiar in towns and cities, and their chirruping song is a common garden sound. House sparrows nest under the eaves of buildings even in the centre of a busy city. Other sparrows occupy a huge range of habitats – swamp sparrows in swamps, fox sparrows in forests, sage sparrows in deserts, and song sparrows in scrubland. Some sparrows are called buntings and these tend to be more brightly coloured, especially the male indigo bunting, painted bunting and lazuli bunting.

NUTCRACKER BEAKS

Finches of various kinds, with their powerful seed-cracking beaks, are found throughout the world. They often visit bird tables for extra food, especially in winter. The chaffinch is one of Europe's most common birds, nesting in a wide range of wooded habitats. Goldfinches, with their attractive red, gold and black plumage, often feed in small flocks on the seed heads of thistles or teasels. The powerful bill of the hawfinch can even crush cherry stones with ease. The tips of the crossbill's beak actually cross over at the tip. This allows the bird to extract seeds from pine cones.

◄ The snow bunting nests further north than any other land bird. It also breeds on high mountains, where its black and white plumage gives good camouflage among the rocks and ice.

◘ The snow bunting ranges into the Arctic Circle, and also up near the summits of the world's highest mountains. A species of bunting is found almost everywhere in the world, from the Equator nearly to the Poles.

INSIDE A BIRD

No birds have teeth, so they cannot chew their food. This means the inner parts must grind and mash the food into a pulp. This happens in a muscular, strong-walled section of the digestive system called the gizzard. First, the swallowed food enters a stretchy storage bag in the chest region, called the crop. A bird can feed very fast, fill its crop, and then digest its food more slowly later. It can also carry food back to its nest in the crop, and bring it up (regurgitate it) for its young.

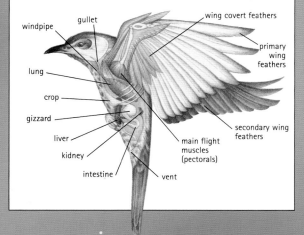

windpipe, gullet, wing covert feathers, primary wing feathers, lung, crop, gizzard, liver, kidney, intestine, vent, main flight muscles (pectorals), secondary wing feathers

Hawfinches are big, orange-brown finches that live in broadleaved trees, such as beech or hornbeam, across most of Europe and Asia. The thick, strong beak can crack open nuts and even the seed stones of fruits such as cherries. The hawfinch is very shy. It is often only glimpsed in the treetops when it is feeding or when it makes its loud "tik" call.

EXPERT WEAVERS

Weaver birds are related to sparrows and are similar in body shape. But most are larger and more colourful than sparrows, with yellow, black and red plumage – especially in the males. Weavers make the most complex nests of any bird. Even the simplest designs have long funnels or tubes at the nest entrance to keep out predators (and cuckoos).

The song of the corn bunting sounds like a bunch of jangling keys. This bird is found in farmland and similar open areas.

The sociable weavers of Africa work together to build the most elaborate constructions in the bird world. Their huge colonial nest looks like the thatched roof of a cottage, transported to the branches of a tree. Each pair of weavers has its own entrance on the underside of the nest. The whole multi-nest may measure more than 7 m across. Village weavers also build a colonial nest from intertwined grass stems, with up to 100 nest compartments inside.

MORE PERCHING BIRDS:

Buntings
• 552 species
Finches
• 155 species
Weavers
• 95 species
Sparrows
• 35 species

99

⬓ Blue whales emit ear-splitting,
low-pitched grunts that are the
loudest noises made by any animal.

SECTION 7
MAMMALS

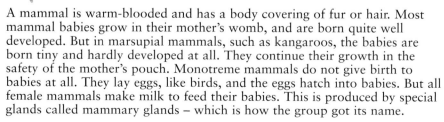

FOR MANY PEOPLE, THE MOST FAMILIAR GROUP OF ANIMALS IS THE MAMMALS. This is partly because we keep many kinds of mammals as pets and on farms, including dogs, cats, rabbits, horses, cows, sheep and pigs. Also, the best-known animal in the world, and one of the most numerous, is a mammal – the human being.

A mammal is warm-blooded and has a body covering of fur or hair. Most mammal babies grow in their mother's womb, and are born quite well developed. But in marsupial mammals, such as kangaroos, the babies are born tiny and hardly developed at all. They continue their growth in the safety of the mother's pouch. Monotreme mammals do not give birth to babies at all. They lay eggs, like birds, and the eggs hatch into babies. But all female mammals make milk to feed their babies. This is produced by special glands called mammary glands – which is how the group got its name.

There are some 4,000 kinds, or species, of mammal. They include the largest creature ever to live on Earth, the blue whale. Most mammals walk and run on land. However, the whales, dolphins, porpoises and sea cows spend all their lives in water. Another group of mammals, the bats, have taken to the air. Others, such as moles and mole rats, tunnel underground and rarely see the light of day.

EGG-LAYING MAMMALS

PERHAPS THE ODDEST OF ALL MAMMALS ARE THE MONOTREMES, OR EGG-LAYING MAMMALS. There are only three kinds – the platypus and two species of echidnas or spiny anteaters, the short-beaked and long-beaked echidnas. They all live in Australia or nearby New Guinea. The platypus is also called the duck-billed platypus, because its mouth is shaped like a duck's beak. These highly unusual mammals do not give birth to babies, like the other 4,000-plus mammal species. The females lay eggs, like a bird or reptile.

◻ The short-beaked echidna grows to about 35 cm in length. Both long- and short-beaked echidnas have strong claws for digging up their prey and excavating nest burrows.

STICKY TONGUE
The echidnas look similar to porcupines, being covered with long, sharp, protective spines. They use their powerful front claws to dig into soil, or ant or termite nests. Then they lick up the prey using their long, sticky tongue.

◻ The long-beaked echidna grows to about 28 inches (70 cm) in length.

The female echidna keeps her single egg in a temporary brood pouch which develops on her belly. The egg hatches after about ten days. Then she feeds the tiny, helpless baby on her milk, as other mammals do.

The short-beaked echidna is quite common in Australia and New Guinea. It is found in a wide range of habitats, from dry deserts to cold uplands, scrubland and forest. The long-beaked echidna is found only in the highlands of New Guinea. It is larger than its short-beaked cousin, with fur longer than the spines, and a longer, down-curved snout. Despite its name of spiny anteater, this echidna feeds mostly on earthworms, which it catches using the tough spines on its tongue.

THE PLATYPUS
The platypus lives in eastern Australia, including Tasmania. It is one of the strangest of all mammals. When a preserved platypus body was first studied by scientists in 1798, they thought it was a fake made of several animals sewn together. The platypus has a wide beak like a duck, a flattened tail like a beaver and webbed feet like an otter.

◻ The female platypus digs a very long breeding burrow, 18 m or more into the riverbank. At the end of the burrow she makes a nest of dry leaves and grass.

INSIDE A MAMMAL
All mammals have the same basic parts inside. The body has an internal skeleton made of bones, which give strength and support. In the chest are the heart and lungs. The abdomen contains the digestive, waste-disposal and reproductive parts.

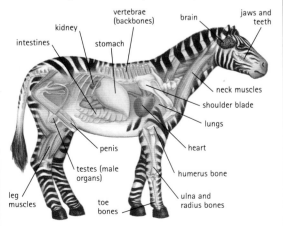

- vertebrae (backbones)
- brain
- jaws and teeth
- kidney
- intestines
- stomach
- neck muscles
- shoulder blade
- lungs
- penis
- heart
- testes (male organs)
- humerus bone
- leg muscles
- toe bones
- ulna and radius bones

⬛ The male platypus has a poison spur hidden in the fur on each hind leg. If threatened, he kicks out and causes the attacker great pain.

WOW! ⚠

The mouth of a long-beaked echidna is just a small slit at the end of the snout. The tongue can poke out 18 cm beyond the snout tip. The echidna has no teeth. It squashes its tiny prey between its tongue and the roof of its mouth.

These body features make it ideally suited to swimming, and a platypus spends up to half its time nosing and grubbing in the water for food. It uses its tail as a rudder and to store a reserve of fat for the winter, when food is often scarce.

ELECTRIC BILL

Platypuses are not often seen since they live along creeks, rivers and lakes, and are usually active at night. They have an extraordinary method of feeding. They hunt at night along the stream or lake bed, detecting prey hidden in the mud by the tiny electrical impulses given out by the muscles in the prey's body. The platypus does this using its wide, leathery bill. This is very sensitive to touch and movements, and also has tiny pits which can detect electricity, like some fish. As it hunts, the platypus keeps its eyes and nostrils tightly closed.

The platypus catches mainly insect grubs, worms, little shrimps and similar small freshwater creatures. It stores them in its cheek pouches and eats them later, when it returns to its burrow in the bank. Then the platypus grinds up its food using horny ridges in its jaws since, like the echidnas, it has no teeth.

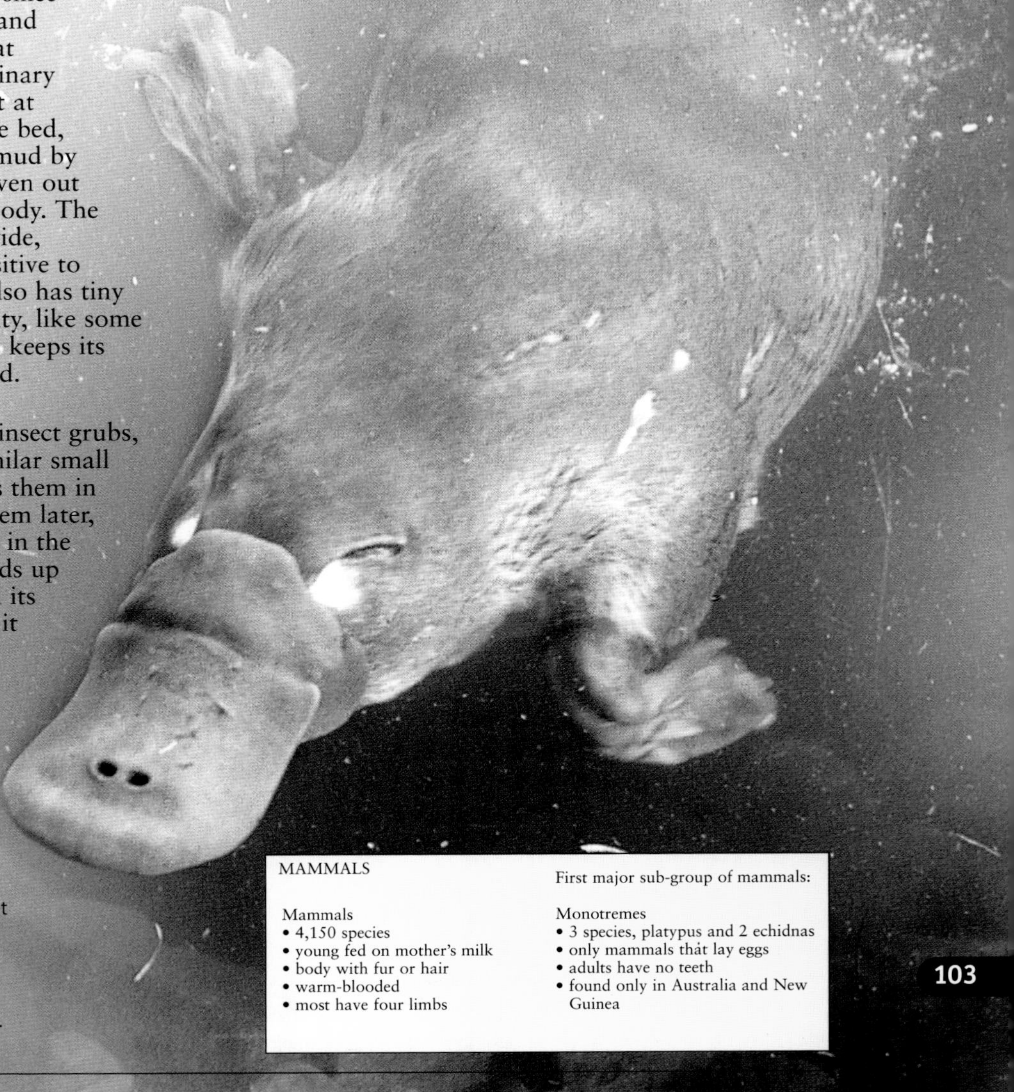

⬛ The platypus catches small creatures including frogs and fish, and even water plants. Each dive lasts about one minute. The head and body are about 45 cm long, and the tail 15–20 cm. Once very rare, platypuses are now protected by law and have become more common in some regions.

MAMMALS	First major sub-group of mammals:
Mammals • 4,150 species • young fed on mother's milk • body with fur or hair • warm-blooded • most have four limbs	Monotremes • 3 species, platypus and 2 echidnas • only mammals that lay eggs • adults have no teeth • found only in Australia and New Guinea

103

MARSUPIAL MAMMALS

MARSUPIALS ARE POUCHED MAMMALS, NAMED AFTER THE POUCH (MARSUPIUM) OF THE FEMALE.

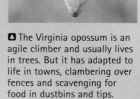

She gives birth to babies that are at a very early stage of development, tiny and helpless. The babies crawl to the pouch and continue to develop there in safety, feeding on her milk. There are about 120 species of marsupial in Australia, 50 species in New Guinea and 90 species in South and Central America. One species, the Virginia opossum, has spread through southern North America. The largest marsupials are kangaroos and wallabies. They have big, muscular hind legs and bound along at great speed.

◪ The marsupial mole has shiny golden fur.

◪ The Virginia opossum is an agile climber and usually lives in trees. But it has adapted to life in towns, clambering over fences and scavenging for food in dustbins and tips.

◧ The female red kangaroo is smaller than the male, weighing less than 30 kg. The young in the pouch is called a joey.

The babies of marsupial mammals are born tiny and undeveloped. At birth, a baby kangaroo is hardly larger than a grape, and its legs have only just begun to grow. Even so, it can crawl from the birth opening to its mother's pouch, where its mouth latches onto her nipple to suck her milk. The baby lives like this for six months. As it grows larger, it begins to leave the pouch for short periods. Meanwhile another tiny, newborn baby arrives. Even when a youngster is more than a year old, it may dash back to the safety of its mother's pouch if danger appears, and still pokes its head in to feed on her milk. Most kangaroos and wallabies eat leaves, stems and shoots. And the smaller, shorter-legged tree kangaroos really do live in trees!

◪ The Tasmanian devil has a body length of about 60 cm. It lives on the Australian island of Tasmania. Its massive teeth and jaws easily crunch bones.

THE APPEALING KOALA

The koala is one of the most appealing marsupials, looking like a teddy bear soft toy. In fact it has very sharp claws to cling on to the branches of the gum (eucalyptus) trees where it lives. So it can give a deep scratch if threatened. Koalas spend much of their lives either sleeping or munching on gum leaves. They get all their nourishment and moisture from these, so they rarely come down to the ground. Another bear-like marsupial is the wombat. It lives in a complex system of burrows and chambers, which it digs using its powerful, large-clawed feet.

◨ Wombats feed on roots, shoots and other plant material. They sometimes raid farm crops.

MARSUPIAL VERSIONS

There are many other kinds of marsupial. Some resemble mammals living on other continents. For example, there are marsupial mice and marsupial cats or quolls.

◄ The brushtail possum once lived in forests, but has now spread to Australian suburbs, where it eats food scraps.

▸ One of the smallest marsupials is the honey possum. It is about the same size as a house mouse and lives on nectar and pollen from flowers. The possum licks up its food using its long, bristly, brush-tipped tongue.

There are also marsupial shrews or planigales, rat- and rabbit-like marsupials called bandicoots, and even marsupial moles. The pouches of tunnelling marsupials, such as the wombat and marsupial mole, open backwards, so they do not fill with earth as the female digs her way through the ground.

MARSUPIAL GLIDERS

Several species of marsupials can swoop from tree to tree, using wing-like flaps of skin stretched between the front and rear limbs. These include various types of gliders, and the pygmy possum or feathertail glider. The greater glider, which weighs 1.4 kg, can travel as far as 91 m in a single burst of "flight".

Creatures very similar to marsupial gliders are the colugos or flying lemurs. There are only two species, living in the forests of Malaysia and the Philippines. They swoop through the air in a similar way to marsupial gliders, but with better flight control, covering more than 150 m. However, these animals are not marsupial mammals, they are placental mammals.

About 20 species of Australian marsupials have become extinct during the last 200 years. Dozens more are threatened, mainly by habitat loss or competition from introduced animals. The mahogany glider, however, was believed to be extinct, but has been rediscovered in the forests of North Queensland.

The second major sub-group of mammals:

Marsupials
• about 270 species
• tiny young raised in mother's pouch
• live mainly in Australia, New Guinea, South and Central America

Marsupial groups include:

American opossums
• 75 species
Marsupial mice
• 53 species

Kangaroos and wallabies
• 50 species
Bandicoots
• 17 species
Ringtail possums
• 16 species
Brushtail possums and cuscuses
• 14 species
Rat kangaroos
• 10 species
Gliders
• 7 species
Pygmy possums
• 7 species

Shrew (rat) opossums
• 7 species
Wombats
• 3 species
Bilbies
• 2 species
Honey possum
• 1 species
Koala
• 1 species
Marsupial mole
• 1 species
Monito del monte
• 1 species
Numbat
• 1 species

▾ Koalas look peaceful and quiet. But they can defend themselves with their sharp claws, and the bellowing call of the male koala can be heard over a distance of several kilometres. Koalas are a threatened species and are fully protected.

BATS

ABOUT ONE-QUARTER OF ALL MAMMAL SPECIES ARE BATS. They are the biggest mammal group, after rodents. About 960 different species are found throughout the world, except in the coldest regions. Although some mammals can glide, bats are the only mammals that can truly fly. There are two main kinds of bats. One is the fruit bats and flying foxes. These are mostly large, with a body the size of a small dog and wings about 1.8 m across. They eat fruits, flowers, leaves and other plant parts. The other main kind is the insect-eating bats. These are much smaller, with a body the size of a mouse or rat. Surprisingly, some insect-eating bats not only eat insects, but also mice, voles, frogs and fish.

⬧ The vampire bat has four razor-like canine teeth. It makes only a tiny slit in its victim's skin. It usually chooses a furless or featherless part of the body, such as the ankle. It feeds for about half an hour each night. In some areas vampire bats spread diseases such as rabies.

Most bats are nocturnal, or active at night. Apart from flying foxes, they find their way by a sound-radar system called echolocation. Most smaller bats feed on night-flying insects such as moths. But some bats specialize in finding other foods. The fisherman bat of Central and South America swoops over rivers and lakes, and hooks up fish from just under the surface.

⬧ The pipistrelle is one of the smallest bats, with a head and body 4 cm long and a wingspan of 20 cm.

lower arm bone (radius) · first finger (thumb) · claw · second finger · wrist · third finger · wing membrane (patagium) · fifth finger · fourth finger

A BAT'S WING

The wing (arm) of a bat is different from the wing of a bird. It is a thin, skin-like membrane, the patagium, stretched between hugely long arm, hand and finger bones. The patagium is a thin layer of blood vessels and elastic threads sandwiched between two layers of skin.

⬧ The mouse-eared bat's high-pitched squeaks of sound emerge from its mouth. Some bats emit sounds through the nose.

outgoing pulse of ultrasound

It uses its long, curved claws to spear the fish. Mastiff bats catch bees and wasps. Greater horseshoe bats, named after their horseshoe-shaped noses, dive onto beetles and other ground-dwelling insects. Other bats catch night-flying birds such as nightjars and even small owls.

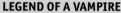

⬛ The huge ears of long-eared bats can turn and swivel with great accuracy, like radar dishes. They catch the returning echoes of sound, which a bat uses to find its way in the dark.

⬛ Resting, or roosting, bats hang upside down by their foot claws. They wrap their wings around the body to keep in warmth.

⬛ Flying foxes like the common long-tongued fruit bat have dog- or fox-like faces. They roost by day in trees, often making chattering noises.

LEGEND OF A VAMPIRE

Vampire bats feed on blood. But they are not dangerous to people, as the legends say. Vampire bats live in Central and South America, and are quite small, with a head and body length of only 8 cm. They usually feed on the blood of sleeping cattle, pigs or horses. The vampire bat lands near its victim, crawls over the ground and makes a small slit-like wound in the animal with its sharp teeth. Then it dribbles spit to stop the blood clotting and licks up the oozing blood.

⬛ Some bats catch prey in their tail membranes, others in their foot claws.

Many bats roost together in colonies, in caves or hollow trees, and also inside modern "caves" such as church towers and mine shafts. In tropical areas bats are active all year. In temperate lands, most bats hibernate through the winter, emerging from their deep sleep when the weather warms up again in spring.

The biggest group of bats is the common or vesper bats. It includes common European species such as the pipistrelle, long-eared bat and noctule. The smallest mammal is a bat – Kitti's hog-nosed bat from Thailand. Its head and body are just 3 cm long and it weighs 1.5 g. And one of the biggest gatherings of mammals is of bats. Some colonies of the Mexican free-tailed bat contain up to 10 million bats, all clustered together in a single cave.

HOW BATS FLY IN THE DARK

returning echo

Most bats use echolocation to find their way, even in total darkness. They emit very high-pitched pulses of sound, called ultrasound, which are too high for most humans to hear. The sound pulses bounce back as echoes off nearby objects. The bat hears the pattern of echoes and analyses it to give a "sound-picture" of the surroundings. Flying foxes and fruit bats have good eyesight and smell, and fly mainly at dusk and dawn. Most do use echolocation.

BATS	Some groups of bats:	
• 960 species		Sheath-tailed bats
• the only mammals with true, powered flight	Flying foxes, fruit bats • 175 species	• 50 species Slit-faced bats • 12 species
• front limbs are wings	Common or vesper bats • 320 species	Ghost-faced bats • 8 species
• most are nocturnal	Spear-nosed bats • 140 species	Vampire bats • 3 species
	Free-tailed bats • 90 species	Bulldog bats • 2 species
	Horseshoe bats • 70 species	Hog-nosed bat • 1 species
	Leaf-nosed bats • 60 species	

ANTEATERS, SLOTHS AND ARMADILLOS

SOME MAMMALS LIVE AT A SLOW PACE. They include anteaters, armadillos, pangolins and especially sloths. These creatures share other features too, such as long, sharp claws and very small teeth, or none at all. They feed on soft or tiny food items that do not need much biting or chewing. For defence, armadillos and pangolins have a covering of bands or scales made from tough bone and horn, like a suit of armour. Sloths rely on staying still and unnoticed. Anteaters slash at enemies with their claws.

◖ A sloth is so well suited to hanging around that it can hardly walk on the ground. It has to drag its body along with its curved claws.

LARGEST... !
The largest armadillo is the giant armadillo of Brazil and Peru, at 1.5 m long. It is endangered by the loss of its dense forest habitat.

◪ The tongue of the giant anteater is 60 cm long. It can collect hundreds of termites or ants with a single lick. One anteater may eat 20,000 ants in a single day!

An anteater eats not only ants. It also licks up termites and small grubs with its very long, sticky tongue, which emerges from the small mouth at the end of the long snout. The anteater digs out or rips open the ant nest or termite mound with its large front claws, and licks up the milling insects in their hundreds. But it does not eat them all. It soon moves on, leaving the nest to be repaired as a larder for the future.

◪ The nine-banded armadillo is the most common and widespread type. Like the others, it feeds mainly at night.

◪ The tree pangolin has a gripping or prehensile tail. A rough, scaleless patch of skin on the underside near the tip helps to give extra grip.

The giant anteater is the largest of the four anteater species. It is 200 cm long, but much of this is its long, down-curved nose and brush-like tail. It also has a shaggy coat and an awkward, rolling way of walking. Giant anteaters roam forests and scrub in Central and South America. The other three species are smaller and stay mainly in trees, using the strong tail as an extra limb to clasp branches.

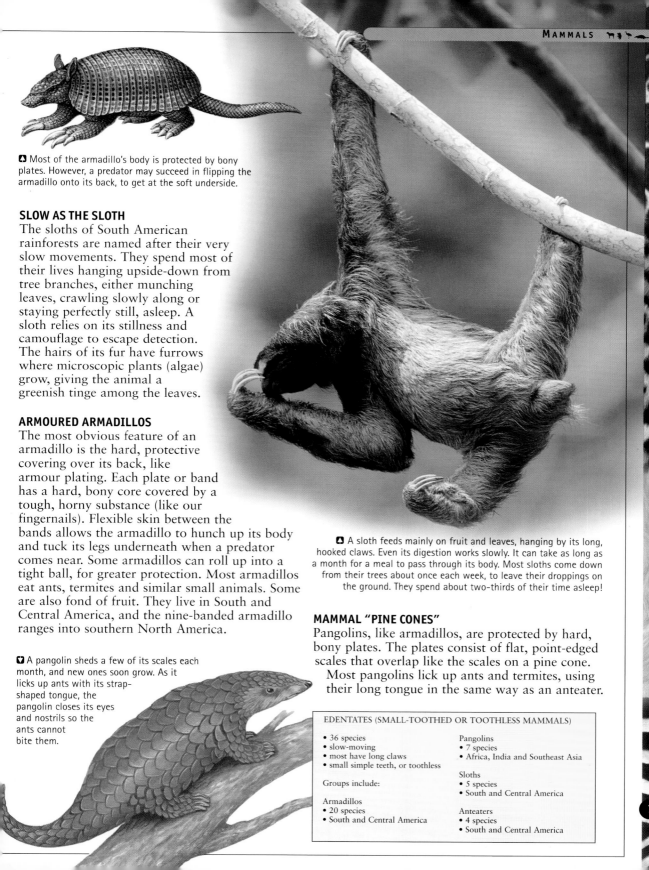

◪ Most of the armadillo's body is protected by bony plates. However, a predator may succeed in flipping the armadillo onto its back, to get at the soft underside.

SLOW AS THE SLOTH
The sloths of South American rainforests are named after their very slow movements. They spend most of their lives hanging upside-down from tree branches, either munching leaves, crawling slowly along or staying perfectly still, asleep. A sloth relies on its stillness and camouflage to escape detection. The hairs of its fur have furrows where microscopic plants (algae) grow, giving the animal a greenish tinge among the leaves.

ARMOURED ARMADILLOS
The most obvious feature of an armadillo is the hard, protective covering over its back, like armour plating. Each plate or band has a hard, bony core covered by a tough, horny substance (like our fingernails). Flexible skin between the bands allows the armadillo to hunch up its body and tuck its legs underneath when a predator comes near. Some armadillos can roll up into a tight ball, for greater protection. Most armadillos eat ants, termites and similar small animals. Some are also fond of fruit. They live in South and Central America, and the nine-banded armadillo ranges into southern North America.

◪ A pangolin sheds a few of its scales each month, and new ones soon grow. As it licks up ants with its strap-shaped tongue, the pangolin closes its eyes and nostrils so the ants cannot bite them.

◪ A sloth feeds mainly on fruit and leaves, hanging by its long, hooked claws. Even its digestion works slowly. It can take as long as a month for a meal to pass through its body. Most sloths come down from their trees about once each week, to leave their droppings on the ground. They spend about two-thirds of their time asleep!

MAMMAL "PINE CONES"
Pangolins, like armadillos, are protected by hard, bony plates. The plates consist of flat, point-edged scales that overlap like the scales on a pine cone.
Most pangolins lick up ants and termites, using their long tongue in the same way as an anteater.

EDENTATES (SMALL-TOOTHED OR TOOTHLESS MAMMALS)

- 36 species
- slow-moving
- most have long claws
- small simple teeth, or toothless

Groups include:

Armadillos
- 20 species
- South and Central America

Pangolins
- 7 species
- Africa, India and Southeast Asia

Sloths
- 5 species
- South and Central America

Anteaters
- 4 species
- South and Central America

RABBITS, HARES AND PIKAS

EVER ALERT TO DANGER, RABBITS AND HARES ARE ALWAYS READY TO DASH FOR SAFETY. They live in open, grassy country, and have large eyes and huge ears to look and listen for predators. Their back legs are long and muscular, ideal for running at high speed from danger. Although they resemble rodents such as squirrels and rats, rabbits and hares belong to a different mammal group, the lagomorphs. This name means "leaping shape", which is what these creatures do to survive. The lagomorph group also includes pikas. These are like small, dumpy rabbits with shorter ears and little legs. They also lack the rabbit's bobtail.

The winter fur of Arctic and snowshoe hares is white, for camouflage in snow and ice. It moults in spring. The summer fur is brown.

The volcano rabbit lives only on grassy mountain slopes in Mexico. It has short ears and a small tail. It is a very rare species, and protected by law.

The hare's prominent eyes allow it to see above and even behind itself, so it can spot predators such as eagles from almost any direction.

There is no exact difference between rabbits and hares. Generally, the larger types with longer legs and longer ears are known as hares, or jackrabbits in North America. The smaller species with shorter ears are usually called rabbits. Hares that live in the far north, such as the Arctic and snowshoe hares, moult into a white coat during the snowy winter season. The numbers of snowshoe hares living in the northern forests of North America vary on a fairly regular cycle.

⚊ "Mad March hares" are usually males battling for a female at breeding time in spring. Or the pawing and boxing hare may be a jill (female) chasing away an unwanted jack (male).

may have up to 20 babies each year, rabbits have a deserved reputation of increasing numbers very quickly.

HAY FOR WINTER
Pikas look like a combination of rabbit and guinea pig or vole. They live in mountainous country in Asia, with one species also in northwest North America. Most pikas prefer rocky slopes. The large-eared pika of the Himalayas and nearby mountains is one of the highest-living mammals, found at heights of more than 6,000 m. Pikas graze on a range of plants, mostly grasses, flowers and young stems. In the autumn, they pull hay, soft twigs and other stores of food into their burrows to eat during the long, cold winter.

⚊ The American black-tailed jackrabbit is actually a type of hare. It uses its large ears to listen for danger and also to keep cool in the great heat of summer.

They reach a peak roughly every ten years, then fall again. Why this is so is not clear. But it affects the populations of lynx, snowy owls and other predators in the same way, since they depend on the hares for food.

The large ears of a rabbit or hare not only pick up the faintest noises, like an elephant's ears; they also help to lose body heat into the air during very hot weather. If a rabbit or hare detects danger, it races away, propelled by great leaps of its large back legs. It may thump the ground first with its rear feet to warn others nearby, and it can zigzag at great speed. Some hares sprint at more than 80 km/h. However, they do not have great stamina, and predators such as wolves soon tire them out with chasing.

GNAWING TEETH
Rabbits and hares have strong teeth for gnawing grasses, stems, seeds, roots, bark and other plant foods. Some rabbits live in groups or colonies in networks of underground tunnels, called warrens, which they dig in the soil of hedges and banks. Most hares live alone and rest in the open, in shallow bowl-like areas in the grass or scrub, called forms. They also have their babies in these forms. For this reason, young hares (known as leverets) can run and hide almost as soon as they are born.

BREEDING LIKE RABBITS
Baby rabbits born in the safety of the breeding chamber or "stop", are blind and helpless at first. Their eyes open at a week old and they venture out of the nest at three weeks. But at only four months of age they can breed. Since one female

⚊ The running hare kicks off with its long back legs, and cushions its landing on the two front legs with paws held together. Then it thrusts its rear legs forwards on either side of the front paws and makes another leap.

⚊ Most pikas, like the northern pika, are about 20–25 cm long.

Rabbits and hares
• 44 species
• large ears
• long back legs
• eyes face sideways
• very short "bob" tail
• slit-like nostrils
• eat plants

Pikas
• 14 species
• rounded ears
• almost tailless
• eat plants

111

MICE, RATS AND CAVIES

◓ The jerboa has huge back feet that work like sandshoes, stopping it from sinking into the desert surface.

THE RODENTS OR GNAWING MAMMALS ARE BY FAR THE LARGEST MAMMAL GROUP. The 1,700 species mean that almost one of every two mammals is a rodent. About seventy-five per cent of these are types of mice and rats, and their South American relatives, cavies – the best-known being the guinea pig. The rodent's key feature is its four long, sharp, chisel-like incisor teeth at the front of the mouth. These can chew even the hardest foods, such as nuts or tree bark. Some small rodents, including mice, rats, hamsters, gerbils and guinea pigs, are often kept as pets. (More rodents are described on pages 114 to 115.)

◓ A dormouse may hibernate for up to eight months, depending on the climate of the region.

◓ The cavy group of rodents includes guinea pigs, porcupines, spiny rats and mole rats.

Mice and rats range in size from the pygmy mouse, at less than 10 cm long including its tail, to rats that reach a total length of 80 cm. The harvest mouse is one of the smallest, with a body hardly larger than a thumb. It is a very agile climber and uses its long tail as an extra limb to grasp grass stems. It spread rapidly when people began to plant wheat and similar crops. But then it suffered as machines took over harvesting from people. It could not escape from its ball-shaped nest as the combine harvester approached.

Some mice and rats have taken to living near people, especially in our houses, farms and food stores. They cause damage and also spread diseases. The fleas that live on certain rats may bite people and spread plague. House mice get into kitchens and food cupboards. Brown and roof rats are a nuisance in grain stores.

Lemmings have blunt noses, small ears, rounded bodies and thick fur. These features help them stay warm in their cold northern homelands. They live among grasses and bushes on the ground, feeding on roots and shoots. When conditions are good and food is plentiful, lemmings breed so fast that they end up eating all of the available food.

◓ The yellow-necked mouse is common in farmland and woods across Europe. It may even come into houses in the autumn, to escape the cold and look for food. It eats mainly seeds, berries and insects.

Once the food supplies have gone, many lemmings set off on a mass migration to find new places to live. During these "lemming years", they become bold and aggressive. At first they travel only at night. But soon they journey by day too. The urge to move on is so strong that they enter towns and cross streets, and even dive into rivers or tumble off cliffs. These migrations have led to legends that the lemmings really want to die!

BIG CHEEKS

The hamster is a familiar pet, yet it is rarely seen in the wild. Its original home was the steppe grasslands of eastern Europe, but it has now spread into central Europe too. Hamsters eat many foods. They carry what they cannot consume back to the nest, filling their stretchy cheek pouches. In the wild, many hamsters hibernate during winter. But they wake up every few days to nibble at their store of nuts, berries and other food.

Another group of small rodents is the jerboas. They have very long back legs and jump exceptionally well, using the long tail to balance.

△ Naked mole rats work together for the good of the colony, like bees or ants. Only the chief female, or queen, can have babies. The rest are "workers" and do specific jobs.

Jerboas live in the deserts of North Africa, the Middle East, and Central Asia. They feed mainly on seeds and insects. Gerbils are similar to jerboas, but they have shorter back legs and smaller ears. Like jerboas, they spend the day in their burrows, to avoid predators and also the intense desert heat.

◁ When lemmings become too numerous in an area, they have a strong instinct to set off and look for less crowded places.

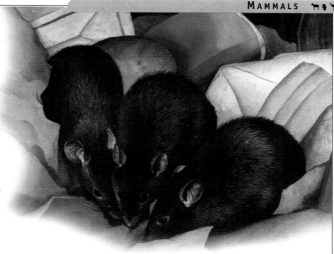

△ Black or ship rats have spread around the world, from their original homeland of tropical Asia. They travel on ships, being agile enough to climb aboard along the mooring ropes.

SLEEPING MICE

Common dormice are about the same size as house mice. But they have soft, light brown fur and a furry tail. They are well known for their long winter sleep or hibernation. The name "dormouse" comes from the French word *dormir*, "to sleep". In summer they eat flowers, shoots, nuts, berries, insects and spiders.

African naked mole rats have hardly any fur and live entirely underground, in large colonies. They chisel through the soil with their huge front teeth. Members of the colony have different jobs. Some are diggers, some gather food, and some guard against intruders. Only one female, the queen, can produce young. Apart from certain insects, this type of colony is unique in the animal world.

△ Jumping mice bound along like miniature kangaroos. They can cover more than 1.8 m in a single leap. Fast reactions and speed help small rodents elude their many predators.

RODENTS
- 1,700 species
- long, sharp gnawing front teeth
- most are small and nocturnal

Some groups of small rodents:

Old World rats and mice
- 480 species
New World rats and mice
- 365 species
Pocket mice
- 65 species
Spiny rats
- 55 species

Jerboas
- 31 species
Jumping mice and birch mice
- 14 species
Dormice
- 10 species
African mole rats
- 9 species
Cane rats
- 2 species
Chinchilla rats
- 2 species
Rock rat
- 1 species

113

LARGE RODENTS

PORCUPINES, BEAVERS, CHINCHILLAS AND COYPUS ARE ALL LARGE RODENTS, BUT THE BIGGEST OF ALL IS THE CAPYBARA OF SOUTH AMERICA. The size of a sheep, the capybara lives in forests near lakes and rivers, and feeds on waterside vegetation. It has partly webbed toes and spends much of its time wading and swimming. The American beaver is another huge rodent, with a head and body about 1m long, and webbed feet suited to life in water. The crested porcupine of Africa is large too, with a head and body about 80 cm long. Like other porcupines, it is protected by spines which are thicker, sharper versions of normal mammal fur.

🔼 The tree porcupine has long toe claws and a muscular, curly, prehensile tail for gripping branches.

🔼 In the wild, chinchillas live in multi-family groups of about 50–100. They eat almost any kind of plant food.

🔽 Young capybaras can run and swim a few hours after birth. Capybaras live in family groups and feed mainly at dusk and dawn. They are preyed on by large cats, especially jaguars, and big snakes such as anacondas.

BEAVERS

Beavers gnaw through trunks to fell trees. They feed on the soft, sap-rich bark. They also use the logs and branches to build a wall or dam across a stream. Then they construct their home or lodge in the pool that forms behind the dam. The lodge gives protection against winter weather and predators such as wolves. Both dam and lodge are strengthened and cemented with stones and mud. The lodge has several tunnels leading from the living quarters down into the water. It also has a "chimney" leading upwards for fresh air. In cold weather, the beaver family stays in the lodge. They feed on twigs, bark and leaves which they have stored in the lodge or jammed under stones in their pool.

◨ Inside a beaver's lodge, a mother suckles her young. When they reach two years of age, they will leave and build their own lodges.

◁ Coypus can cause damage because they raid farm crops and dig burrows in the banks of drainage channels.

The beaver has a unique feature among rodents: its flat, scaly, paddle-like tail. This has two main uses. When the beaver swims with its webbed back feet, the tail is used as a rudder for steering. If the beaver senses danger, it slaps its tail onto the water's surface with a loud splash, to warn others of its family group.

PORCUPINES

There are two main groups of porcupines. The American or New World porcupines live mainly in trees and most have prehensile tails. They feed on leaves, fruits and shoots, feeding mostly at night. The Old World porcupines of Europe, Africa and Asia are ground-dwellers. At night they grub about in the soil for roots and other plant food. They also feed on fruits and berries, and can damage crops. By day, they sleep in their burrows.

Porcupines cannot "shoot" their spines, or quills, at enemies. Instead, they rush at an attacker and turn around to jab in the spines. If the spines

▶ The biggest spines on the crested porcupine's back are 30 cm long. This rodent rattles special hollow tail spines as a warning that it may charge backwards at an attacker.

▶ The beaver's sharp gnawing teeth, the incisors, can cut down a small tree in a few minutes.

pierce the skin, they come away from the porcupine's body and work into the flesh.

CAVIES

Among the South American cavy group there are several large species. The mara of Argentina has a head and body up to 75 cm long, and very long legs. It grazes in open grassland and can outrun most predators, sprinting at 45 km/h. Agoutis are also large cavies. They look like giant, tailless rats. They feed by day on plants and rest at night in burrows. An agouti can leap over 2 m straight upwards to avoid danger.

Another group of cavies is the chinchillas and viscachas. The chinchilla itself is now rare in its natural habitat, the rocky uplands of the Andes mountains. But it is commonly kept as a pet, and some are still farmed for their fur, which is the finest and softest of any mammal. In the wild, this fur keeps the chinchilla warm in the bitter Andean winter, and is kept in good condition by regular dust baths.

The coypu is another large rodent of the cavy group. Swimming, it looks similar to a beaver, but has a rat-like tail. It eats water plants and rests by day in tunnels.

▶ Maras are active by day. They search for any type of plant material to eat, including grass, shoots, leaves and fruits. They can run almost as fast as a hare, bounding along in a similar manner using their strong back legs.

OLDEST... !
Porcupines are among the longest-lived rodents. The oldest known individual was at least 27 years of age when it died in a zoo. Since porcupines are so well protected by their spines, they may live almost as long in the wild.

MAIN GROUPS OF LARGER RODENTS (continued from page 113):	
Porcupines • 21 species	Pacas • 2 species
Beavers • 2 species	Degus • 8 species
Mountain beaver • 1 species	Tuco-tucos • 33 species
Springhare • 1 species	Gundis • 5 species
Agoutis • 13 species	Chinchillas • 6 species
Hutias • 13 species	Capybara • 1 species
Pacarana • 1 species	Coypu • 1 species

DEER, CAMELS AND PIGS

MAMMALS WITH HOOVES RATHER THAN CLAWS ON THEIR FEET ARE CALLED UNGULATES. There are 203 species, all plant-eaters, in two main groups. The larger group is the even-toed ungulates, with two or four hoofed toes on each foot. They include deer, cattle, antelopes, giraffes, hippos, pigs, camels and llamas. The odd-toed ungulates have one, three or five hooves per foot (page 118). All even-toed ungulates, except pigs and peccaries, have a special form of digestion. The stomach is divided into several chambers. Food goes into the first chamber, the rumen, where it is part-digested. Then the animal brings it up and "chews the cud" before swallowing it again for the rest of digestion.

◄ Giraffes live in scattered flocks that are constantly changing. Often mother and daughter giraffes travel together.

◄ During the breeding season, male deer like this wapiti bellow and threaten rival males for control of the herd. This is called the rut.

Deer are among the most common and widespread hoofed mammals. They live mainly in woods and forests, browsing on leaves. Some, like red and fallow deer, have spread to other habitats, such as moors and parks. Male deer have antlers, which they shed and re-grow each year, and which they use to battle with rival males at breeding time. Only in reindeer, or caribou, do females also have antlers. Deer live in herds for safety, have keen senses, and flee danger at great speed.

Most camels today are domesticated, used as pack animals in dry scrub and desert, and to provide meat, milk, skins and hair. But some wild camels can still be found in the remote grasslands of Mongolia. These are bactrian or two-humped camels. Domestic one-humped or dromedary camels live throughout the Middle East and North Africa.

Some dromedaries were taken to Australia, as pack animals for the inland deserts, and now live wild in the outback.

WOOLLY COUSINS
The llama, alpaca, guanaco and vicuna of South America are close relatives of camels. They live mainly on the slopes of the Andes mountains and have thick, woolly coats. Llamas and alpacas are domesticated, kept as pack animals and for their fine wool. The vicuna is a protected species.

◄ Camels survive for days without food and weeks without a drink. They obtain some moisture from food, and also make water in their bodies because of their specialized body chemistry. A camel can gulp 50 litres in a few minutes.

TALLEST...!
An adult male giraffe may be 6 m tall. And it can poke out its long tongue to reach leaves almost 50 cm higher.

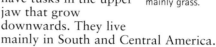

◘ Wild pigs like the warthog use their tusks and strong snouts to grub in the soil for their varied food of roots, bulbs and small animals.

Giraffes are so tall they are easy to spot in their homeland of the African savanna (grassland). They use their great height to reach tasty buds, leaves and fruits in the tree tops. The okapi is a close relative of the giraffe. This extremely shy forest dweller is seldom seen in the wild. It stands almost 1.8 m tall and has a giraffe-like head, neck and body, although the neck is not quite as long in proportion to the body as the giraffe's. It also has striped legs like a zebra.

◘ A fallow deer youngster, or fawn, feeds on its mother's milk.

WILD PIGS

The wild ancestor of our domestic pigs is the wild boar. It has thick fur and a large, powerful head. Wild boars are common in woods and forests in many parts of Europe and Asia. There are another seven species of wild pigs, including the African warthog and the very rare, protected babirusa of Sulawesi in Southeast Asia. Most have tusks formed from their up-curved canine teeth. Peccaries are very similar to wild pigs but have tusks in the upper jaw that grow downwards. They live mainly in South and Central America.

◘ Llamas are South American relatives of camels. They eat mainly grass.

The hippopotamus is the largest even-toed ungulate. Hippos live in Africa, in groups of 10–15. They spend the day lazing in rivers, lakes or water holes. They emerge at night to graze waterside plants, moving along regular pathways. The much smaller pygmy hippo is a rare animal of swampy forests in west and central Africa. It is an endangered species, with just a few thousand left.

◘ The tusks of a hippo are really large canine teeth. They may be 50 cm long. Male hippos sometimes fight each other for females or territory and can inflict nasty wounds with their tusks. Hippos are the third largest land animals. A big male may reach a length of 4 m and weigh well over 3 tonnes.

UNGULATES
• 203 species
• hoofed feet
Even-toed ungulates:
Deer
• 36 species including red, fallow, sika, roe, caribou (reindeer), elk (moose), muntjac
Camels and llamas
• 6 species
Giraffe and okapi
• 2 species
Wild pigs
• 8 species
Peccaries
• 3 species
Hippos
• 2 species
Chevrotains
• 4 species
Musk deer
• 3 species

HORSES, ZEBRAS AND RHINOS

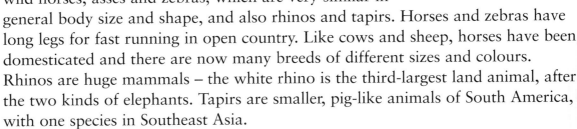

△ An adult tapir has a dark brown coat.

THE HOOFED MAMMALS CALLED ODD-TOED UNGULATES ARE A MUCH SMALLER GROUP THAN THE EVEN-TOED UNGULATES (page 116). They include wild horses, asses and zebras, which are very similar in general body size and shape, and also rhinos and tapirs. Horses and zebras have long legs for fast running in open country. Like cows and sheep, horses have been domesticated and there are now many breeds of different sizes and colours. Rhinos are huge mammals – the white rhino is the third-largest land animal, after the two kinds of elephants. Tapirs are smaller, pig-like animals of South America, with one species in Southeast Asia.

Horses, donkeys, asses and zebras are all known as equids. All domestic horses belong to the species *Equus caballus*. They are probably descended from horses that looked very similar to Przewalski's horse, *Equus przewalskii*, of the Mongolian steppe (grassland) in Central Asia. There are no longer any truly wild

△ A baby Brazilian tapir is born with spots and stripes, but these fade and disappear when it becomes an adult.

members of this species. It was rescued from extinction by being domesticated by local Mongolian people, and being bred in various wildlife parks. It may be possible to re-establish wild herds of Przewalski's horses in their Mongolian homeland.

There are two species of wild ass, one in Africa and one in Asia. Domestic donkeys are descended from a form of the African wild ass. Asses are smaller than horses and have longer ears, a more uneven mane and a tufted tail.

STRIPED HORSES

Zebras are "striped horses". The three species live mainly on the plains of east and southern Africa. Like all equids, zebras live in herds.

◨ No one knows why zebras have such vivid stripes. Each zebra's stripe pattern is unique, so perhaps herd members use the markings to recognize each other.

◨ All rhinos are very similar in appearance. The white or square-lipped rhino (below) has a small hump on its back, just in front of the hips. The exceptionally thick skin of the Indian rhino is creased into deep folds at the shoulders and hips. Rhinos are usually peaceful but if they are threatened they will charge.

◁ Zebras use their speed to flee from large predators such as lions, hunting dogs and hyenas.

All equids have just one large hoofed toe on each foot. Rhinoceroses – rhinos for short – have three hoofed toes per foot. They are bulky animals with very thick skin, almost like armour plating. Unlike horses, rhinos generally live alone and have small eyes and poor sight. But their large ears can pick up the faintest sounds and they also have an excellent sense of smell.

Like all odd-toed ungulates, rhinos are plant-eaters. They graze on tough grasses and scrubby bushes. Both males and females have horns, but these are not true horn or bone, they are made of very tightly packed hairs. The white rhino reaches 4.3 m in head–body length, stands over 1.8 m tall at the shoulder and weighs over 3 tonnes. Smallest of the five species is the Sumatran rhino, which is just 2.5 m in length.

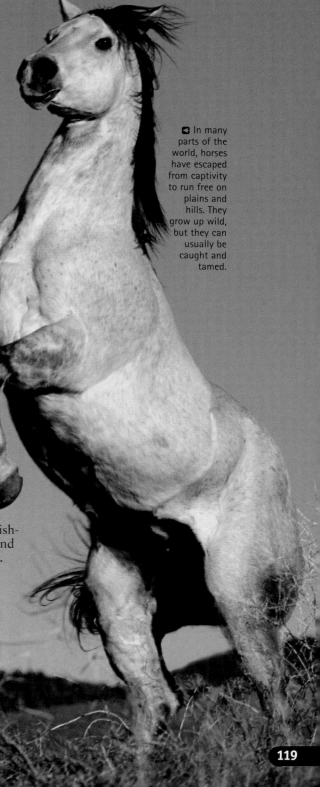

◁ In many parts of the world, horses have escaped from captivity to run free on plains and hills. They grow up wild, but they can usually be caught and tamed.

World Watch

All rhino species are hunted for their horns. Some people believe that the powdered horn has medicinal or magical powers. Horns are also made into trinkets and traditional dagger handles. White rhinos have increased in recent years in protected areas of southern Africa. But the other four species are all very rare. Most threatened is the small Javan rhino. Just a few dozen survive in one or two forest wildlife reserves.

TAPIR "TRUNK"

Tapirs live deep in the tropical forests and swamps of South America and Southeast Asia. They resemble pigs, but without the flat-ended snout. A tapir has a long, flexible upper lip, which it uses to gather food. The South American tapirs are reddish-brown; the Malayan tapir is black and white. All are about 2.5 m in length.

ODD-TOED UNGULATES
(continued from page 117)

Horses, asses and zebras
• 7 species, including domestic horse, Przewalski's horse, African ass, Asiatic ass, Grevy's zebra, mountain zebra, plains zebra

Rhinos
• 5 species, including black rhino, white rhino, Indian rhino, Javan rhino, Sumatran rhino

Tapirs
• 4 species, including Malayan tapir, Brazilian tapir, Baird's tapir, mountain tapir

ELEPHANTS

ELEPHANTS ARE THE LARGEST LAND ANIMALS. AFRICAN ELEPHANTS, WITH THEIR HUGE EARS AND LONGER TUSKS, ARE BIGGER THAN ASIAN ELEPHANTS. These great mammals are famed for their size, strength and stamina, and also for their long lives and complex herd behaviour. People have long trained elephants, especially in Asia, for farming, logging, hunting, warfare and ceremonies. Sadly, people also threaten their survival, especially in Africa, mainly through killing them for their ivory tusks.

World Watch

Elephant tusks are made mainly of a hard, white substance called ivory. This has been treasured through the ages for making tools, ornaments, weapons and decorative carvings. Despite wildlife laws and patrolling wardens, many elephants are still killed illegally for their tusks. However in a few areas where elephants are common, limited legal hunting may be allowed in future.

ELEPHANTS

• 3 species
• African elephant scattered across central, east and southern Africa
• African forest elephant
• Asian elephant found in India, Sri Lanka, Southern China and Southeast Asia (rare in wild)

◪ The Asian elephant has a more domed forehead and humped back than the African elephant. It squirts water, mud or dust over itself to keep cool and to get rid of irritating skin pests.

African elephants live mainly south of the Sahara Desert in a wide range of habitats including grassland, forests and dry, thorny scrub. Asian elephants are found mainly in the forests of India, Sri Lanka and Southeast Asia. Most Asian elephants are kept and trained by people. Fewer than 50,000 live in the wild, in hilly and remote jungle.

◪ Elephants sniff and caress each other when they meet, to make sure that they are from the same herd, not intruders.

In each species, a small family group lives together. They move slowly and steadily, feeding mainly on grasses, bark, leaves and twigs. They spend up to 18 hours feeding and consume about 180 kg of food each day. An elephant walks at an average speed of 5 km/h. However, if it senses danger, it can sprint away or charge at the attacker at up to 40 km/h – which is faster than a human could run away.

Elephants keep in touch with their herd members in several ways. They have a simple language of deep growls and rumbles which carry for hundreds of metres in open country. They also sniff the air with their trunks, and they touch other herd members with their trunks too. In fact the elephant's trunk, an extra-long nose with a flexible tip (one lip in Asian elephants, two in African), has many jobs. It is used for grasping food, squirting water or dust, greeting other elephants and guiding babies or calves.

▶ As drinking holes shrink in the dry season, the herd relies on the long memory of the matriarch (senior female), who may be more than 60 years old. She knows places where there may still be water. The elephants gouge a hole with their tusks and sip the water that collects in it.

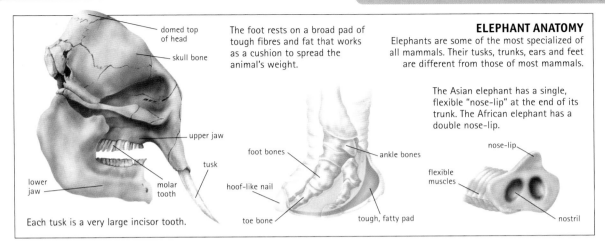

domed top of head

skull bone

The foot rests on a broad pad of tough fibres and fat that works as a cushion to spread the animal's weight.

ELEPHANT ANATOMY

Elephants are some of the most specialized of all mammals. Their tusks, trunks, ears and feet are different from those of most mammals.

upper jaw

The Asian elephant has a single, flexible "nose-lip" at the end of its trunk. The African elephant has a double nose-lip.

foot bones

ankle bones

nose-lip

tusk

lower jaw

molar tooth

hoof-like nail

flexible muscles

Each tusk is a very large incisor tooth.

toe bone

tough, fatty pad

nostril

KEEPING COOL

An elephant cannot drink through its trunk. But it sucks water into the trunk and then squirts the water into its mouth – or over its back for a cooling "shower". Elephants also keep cool by bathing in mud and flapping their ears. The ears work like radiators to lose excess body heat into the air.

OVERSIZED TEETH

An elephant's tusks are its incisor teeth. They start to grow at about two years of age, and continue to grow throughout the animal's life. Both males and females have them, but usually in female Asian elephants they are short and hidden by the trunk and the lower lips.

LARGEST... !

The largest African male elephants stand 4 m tall at the shoulder, measure 10 m from trunk tip to tail tip, and weigh over 6 tonnes. The tusks can be over 3 m long.

◗ An elephant herd is led by the matriarch. She remembers the location of seasonal feeding places.

121

CATS

"CARNIVORE" MEANS "MEAT-EATER".
The Carnivora group includes mammals with long, sharp claws to catch prey and long, sharp teeth to rip it up. This group is described over the next four pages, starting with the most carnivorous of all – the cats. Some carnivores scavenge or eat the occasional fruit or berry. But the cats are active hunters of living prey, with large eyes to see in the dark, and claws which (except for the cheetah) can be pulled back into the toes to keep them sharp. The carnivore group also includes wolves and wild dogs, hyenas, bears, raccoons, pandas, civets, genets, weasels, mongooses and, in the sea, seals and sea lions.

◐ The lynx lives in all northern continents. It is similar to the bobcat (opposite, top right), but larger, with bigger ear and cheek tufts. It takes larger prey such as hares and young deer.

◐ The cheetah is the fastest land animal over short distances. It can reach speeds of more than 95 km/h. But it gives up after about 180 m if the prey seems to be getting away.

◑ A lion pride is led by the chief male. Females or lionesses lack the long neck mane. Cubs lose their spots as they grow.

Cats are found around the world in many habitats, from cold mountains to moist tropical forests. They combine strength and stealth with speed and agility, using their excellent eyesight, hearing and smell.

Cats are a uniform group, which means they are very similar in overall body shape and features – and also in their hunting methods. Most live alone and prowl at night. They stalk their prey quietly, keeping low near the ground. Then they make a quick dash to grab the victim, holding it down with their hooked claws and biting it with their long, sharp canine teeth. The large, sharp-edged cheek teeth or carnassials can shear through tough skin, sinews and gristle.

Lions are the only cats that live and hunt in groups, called prides. The large, shaggy-maned chief male patrols the pride's territory, roaring and leaving scent marks to warn off other prides. The lionesses do the hunting, often as a team to bring down a zebra or wildebeest. One or two lionesses walk towards the victim, to drive it towards the others who are waiting in ambush.

◐ Ocelots range from southern North America down to South America. They are expert swimmers and climbers, catching birds in the trees and frogs in the water.

THE DOG-LIKE CAT

The cheetah is built more like a greyhound than a cat, with a long, flexible back, long slim legs and a relatively small head. It hurls itself after its prey with an amazing burst of speed, rather than stalking. The serval is a smaller version of the cheetah, but has larger ears. It also lives in Africa, hunts by day and races after prey such as hares.

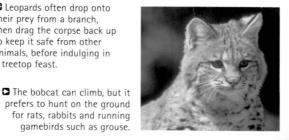

◖ Leopards often drop onto their prey from a branch, then drag the corpse back up to keep it safe from other animals, before indulging in a treetop feast.

◗ The bobcat can climb, but it prefers to hunt on the ground for rats, rabbits and running gamebirds such as grouse.

◗ Tigers are the biggest cats, and the rare Siberian tiger is the biggest of the tigers. It measures 3 m long and weighs over 300 kg.

THE BLACK "PANTHER"

The most adaptable of the seven species of big cat is the leopard. It has short legs and a muscular body, and swims or climbs after its prey. It often prowls near towns and villages and may lie on a branch, ready to drop silently on a victim passing below. Some leopards are born with almost black fur, and are called black panthers. The snow leopard or ounce is slightly smaller than the leopard and has very thick fur, to keep out the cold in its Asian mountain home. It can easily leap across an icy ravine 3 m wide.

SMALLER CATS

There are smaller cats on almost every continent. Most are about 80–110 cm long, including the tail. They live in trees, using the tail to help them balance, and hunt birds, snakes, lizards, squirrels and small monkeys. The pampas cat of South America is at home on grassland, where it pursues rodents and ground birds.

TAME CATS?

The many types of domestic cat were probably bred from the African wild cat, beginning in Egypt some 4,000 years ago. These first domestic cats probably caught mice in grain stores. Pet cats have the night-prowling, hunting instincts of their wild ancestors. In some areas, they have returned to live and breed in the wild, and are called feral cats.

CATS *(felids)*

Big cats
• 7 species
• sharp teeth and claws
• can roar loudly

Lion
• Africa
Tiger
• South and East Asia
Jaguar
• Central and South America
Leopard
• Africa, South Asia
Snow leopard
• Central Asia

Clouded leopard
• Southeast Asia
Cheetah
• Africa, Middle East

Small cats
• 28 species
• resemble big cats, but smaller
• most cannot roar loudly

Small cats include the cougar (puma or mountain lion, the largest small cat), lynx, bobcat, caracal, ocelot, margay, leopard cat, African wild cat, European wild cat, black-footed cat (the smallest small cat)

DOGS, FOXES AND HYENAS

☼ The fennec fox of North Africa hunts small prey such as termites and other insects, mainly by sound, so it has very large ears.

THE DOG FAMILY INCLUDES WOLVES, FOXES AND JACKALS, AS WELL AS THE FAMILIAR DOMESTIC DOG, WHICH WAS PROBABLY BRED FROM THE GREY WOLF. All of these carnivores (page 122) are strong and agile, with long legs for distance running, muscular bodies, powerful sharp-toothed jaws, and keen senses of sight, hearing and especially smell. They differ from cats mainly in that they have longer muzzles, they cannot pull their claws into their toes, and most live in pairs or larger groups called packs – apart from foxes, which dwell alone. Hyenas are also dog-like carnivores, but they are not members of the dog family.

Dogs have a different hunting technique from that of cats. Their long, powerful legs enable them to run well for long distances. They can track prey for many kilometres, following the scent until the prey tires and is caught.

☼ The coyote, with its mournful howl, may live alone but also gathers in packs to hunt.

THE BIGGEST DOG
The grey wolf is the largest of the dog family, with a head–body length of 130 cm.

☼ The grey wolf's strength, stamina and cunning are famed in myth and legend.

☼ The Arctic fox has thick fur that turns white in winter, matching its snowy surroundings.

It is found in remote scrub, forest, tundra and mountains – mainly because people have driven it away. Wolves eat a wide range of meat, from deer to mice, voles and lemmings. They also scavenge, and even take berries and fruits. The coyote is common in parts of North America, and resembles a smaller version of the wolf.

☼ A male, or dog, red fox and a female, or vixen, chase in courtship before mating.

The maned wolf lives in tall grassland in parts of South America. It has red-brown fur and such long, slim legs that it looks like a "wolf on stilts".

⬛ The African wild dog is an endangered species. There are only about 5,000 left, mainly in one Tanzanian wildlife reserve. They are the most efficient of all pack hunters.

THE DOMESTIC DOG

All domestic dogs, from huge great danes to tiny chihuahuas, belong to one species, *Canis familiaris*. The first dogs were probably tamed from a type of grey wolf, as long as 10,000 years ago. The dingo of Australia may once have been an even earlier, part-domesticated form of the wolf. But dingoes now roam wild across large areas of Australia. The most carnivorous dogs are the African wild dogs, whose teeth are particularly large and sharp. They feed mainly on large mammals brought down by a pack of up to 20 members.

WILY CUNNING

Most foxes are agile and stealthy, using a combination of stalking and running to catch prey. The red fox has a legendary reputation for cunning. It adapts to most habitats and foods, including those provided by people, so it has become one of the most

⬛ The striped hyena has a horse-like mane that extends from head to tail. It searches at night for carcasses of large animals already part-eaten by big cats.

widespread of all mammals. In spring and summer it feasts on eggs, young birds and rodents. In the autumn it fattens itself on fruits and berries and takes young rabbits and hares. In winter it raids rubbish bins and tips. Other foxes have similar wide tastes, ranging from crabs and dead fish along the water's edge to worms, beetles, snails, berries and fungi.

⬛ Most dogs bark, yip or yelp. But the dingo of the Australian outback rarely makes a sound.

Jackals are similar to foxes, although slightly larger, with a head–body length of 70–100 cm. They eat a wide range of foods, too. Unlike foxes, jackals live in family groups of four to six members. They hunt as a pack to catch prey such as small gazelles and antelopes.

THE MASTER SCAVENGERS

Hyenas do not belong to the dog family. But they are similar powerful carnivores. Far from slinking away like cowards, hyenas are very aggressive and successful pack-hunters. The hyena has one of the strongest sets of jaws and teeth in the animal kingdom. It is an expert scavenger, helping vultures to clear the remains of dead animals from the African plains. The hyena eats skin, chews gristle and cracks bones with ease. Some hyena groups do hunt and kill more than half their victims. Even lions are wary about trying to take a kill from a pack of hyenas.

⬛ Jackals, like most wild dogs, convey different messages to pack members by the positions of their ears, mouth, legs and tail.

DOGS (canids)
- large, sharp canine teeth
- claws cannot be pulled into toes
- most can bark or yelp

Larger wild dogs
- 4 species

Grey or timber wolf
- All northern lands
Red wolf
- Southeast North America
Coyote
- North and Central America
Dingo
- Australia, Southeast Asia

Other wild dogs
- 5 species including dhole, African wild dog, maned wolf, raccoon dog, bush dog

Jackals
- 4 species
- Africa, Middle East, India

Foxes
- 21 species
- worldwide

Hyenas
- 4 species
- Africa, Middle East

125

BEARS, RACCOONS AND PANDAS

⬥ The tree-dwelling sun bear of Southeast Asia is the smallest bear. It has a head–body length of only 1.2 m.

BEARS ARE NOT ESPECIALLY CARNIVOROUS. They catch prey such as deer, birds and fish. But they also scratch up worms and grubs, raid wild bees' nests for honey and eat buds, fruits, seeds and roots. However, like other carnivores, they have sharp teeth and strong jaws. They are big and muscular, with powerful limbs and huge paws. Raccoons are much smaller and look like a combination of bear and dog. They live across North, Central and South America. The red panda is similar to a raccoon and dwells in eastern Asia. Its cousin is one of the world's rarest yet best-known creatures – the giant panda.

⬥ Asian black bear

⬥ Red panda

◄ Brown bears feast on salmon as they try to leap up waterfalls on their way to their spawning places upstream.

The giant panda is a member of the carnivore group, but it hardly ever eats meat. It consumes mainly stems and leaves of bamboos.

Bears may look friendly and cuddly. But the larger species are massive, powerful animals, and sometimes dangerous to people – especially a mother bear protecting her young. If a bear is disturbed, it may charge as its main method of self-defence. Bears were once hunted for their fur, to protect farm animals and for "sport". Today most species are rare and live in remote places. Because of their unpredictable nature, they are best left undisturbed.

The creamy white fur of the polar bear blends in well with its snowy, icy habitat in the far north. This camouflage helps it to stalk seals on the ice without being detected. As well as very thick fur, polar bears have a thick layer of fat under their skin to keep out the cold. A polar bear can run fast and even catch young or sick reindeer. Like other bears, it has poor eyesight and relies mainly on smell. It can scent a seal or walrus carcass 3 km away.

The kinkajou lives in Central and northern South America. It rests in a tree hole by day and comes out at night to feed on small animals and fruits. Its tail is prehensile, working like a fifth limb to grasp branches.

VARIABLE BEARS

The Asian (Himalayan) black bear has a silky coat with a white V-shaped chest mark and large, rounded ears. It is an expert climber, eats ants and grubs as well as fruits and nuts, and often rests in the branches. The small sun bear lives in the forests of Southeast Asia, where it feeds on fruits, termites, small birds and mammals. The brown bear species is very variable and includes the grizzly, Kodiak and Alaskan bears. The smallest variety is the European brown bear, now very rare, found in a few mountainous regions as far south as Italy and Spain.

The grizzly or brown bear shows its long canine teeth in a warning snarl that few animals will ignore.

The giant panda of China is easily recognized and extremely rare – with perhaps only 1,000 left in the wild. It looks like a bear, but it is not closely related to bears. There is so little goodness in its bamboo food that it eats for up to 15 hours each day. The red panda is related to the giant panda, but is much smaller, fox-like in shape, and with deep red fur.

ABOUT AT NIGHT

The common raccoon, with its "bandit" face mask, is a well-known night-time scavenger in North America. It eats fish, frogs, small birds and mammals, eggs, fruits, nuts, seeds – in fact, almost anything. The raccoon group includes coatis, from the forests of South and Central America. The coati's flexible, elongated nose sniffs out insects and similar small prey on the forest floor.

The common raccoon, like the red fox, is adaptable and comes into cities to scavenge in rubbish. It can climb and swim well, and handles food delicately in its front paws.

BEARS (Ursids)	Raccoons and pandas
• 7 species	• 17 species
• large head, wide face	• mostly long-bodied, bushy-tailed
• poor sight but keen smell	• alert, agile and adaptable
• bulky, sturdy body	• live mainly in trees
• big paws and claws	• Americas, apart from
• very short tail	2 panda species
Polar bear	Main groups of raccoons and pandas:
• Arctic Ocean and far north	
Brown bear	Raccoons
• all northern lands, southern Europe	• 6 species including crab-eating raccoon
American black bear	Coatis
• North America	• 4 species including ringtailed coati, white-nosed coati
Asian black bear	Olingos
• Central and South Asia	• 2 species
Sun bear	Ringtail and cacomistle
• Southeast Asia	• 2 species
Sloth bear	Kinkajou
• India, Sri Lanka	• 1 species
Spectacled bear	Pandas
• South America	• 2 species, giant and red

SEALS, SEA LIONS AND SEA COWS

SEALS, SEA LIONS AND THE WALRUS ARE SUPERBLY ADAPTED TO LIFE IN THE WATER. Unlike whales and dolphins, however, they rarely venture into the open ocean. They usually stay near land because they must come ashore to breed, typically on rocky, isolated coasts or on ice. These mammals are all meat-eaters, taking prey such as fish and squid. Sea cows are large, slow-moving mammals that graze on water plants.

◖ Like all sea mammals, the manatee must come to the surface to breathe.

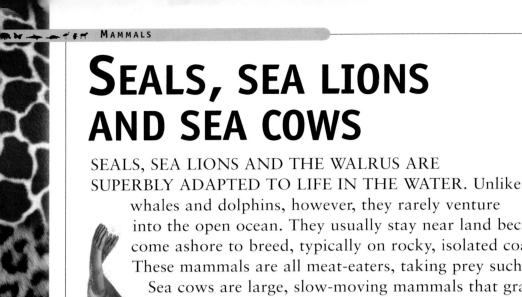

◖ A seal swims by bending its body and pushing with its rear flippers, like a fish uses its tail. The front flippers are held by its sides or used to steer and brake.

Seals, sea lions and sea cows are all marine mammals – they live in the oceans. They all have limbs that are paddle-shaped for rowing themselves through the water. True or earless seals form the largest group, with 19 species. They do have ears, but these lack ear flaps and so are not noticeable on the outside. On land, seals are clumsy and can only slide or hump along slowly. Their rear flippers trail uselessly behind. But in water, few animals can match their speed and grace.

NO CRABS TO EAT
The most abundant seal by far, and one of the world's most numerous large wild mammals, is the crabeater seal. Some 20 million live on and around the pack ice of Antarctica. But it does not eat crabs!

◖ A Galapagos sea lion mother prepares to feed her youngster. Baby seals are called pups.

Crabs do not live in this habitat. Instead, the crabeater, like the great whales, feeds mainly on the tiny shrimp-like krill.

SEAL-EATING SEAL

Three other seals in the same region are the Weddell seal, the smaller Ross seal and the larger leopard seal. The first two dive to great depths, the Weddell seal descending to 450 m after fish and squid. The leopard seal, in contrast, is a sleek, fast and fierce surface predator. It grows to 3.5 m long and pursues mainly penguins, but it will eat large fish and even kill other seals.

◪ Walruses live all around the seas and oceans of the far north. A 4-cm-thick layer of fatty blubber under skin keeps out the intense cold.

◪ The baby harp seal is one of the most appealing of all animals. It gradually loses its fluffy baby fur and develops the dark head, dark side stripes and pale grey background colour of the adult.

FRONT FLIPPER POWER

The eared seals have much more noticeable ear flaps on the sides of the head. They include fur seals and sea lions. They have torpedo-shaped bodies like true seals, but their rear flippers are longer and more mobile, and their front ones larger and more powerful. They swim mainly by "rowing" with these long front flippers. On land, they can shuffle about by tucking their rear flippers under the body and propping themselves up on their front pair. They rest and breed on land at traditional sites called rookeries.

THE SEAL WITH TUSKS

The huge walrus is more than 3 m long. It has a very fat, blubbery body and

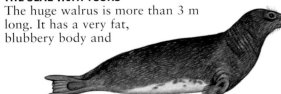

◪ The Mediterranean monk seal is one of the rarest seals, with just a few hundred left. They live in remote sea caves in scattered colonies, in the Mediterranean Sea and Atlantic Ocean.

◪ The male dugong munches sea grass, its body scarred from fights with male rivals at breeding time. A dugong has notched tail flukes like a whale; the manatee's tail is rounded.

extra-long upper canine teeth known as tusks. Both males and females have tusks, which can be 60 cm long. They use the tusks for grubbing in the sea bed for shellfish and other food, and to help pull themselves out from the water.

GENTLE PLANT EATERS

Manatees and dugongs are sometimes called sea cows, because they are peaceful, slow plant-eaters, like cows on land. They graze on water plants in shallow tropical seas and estuaries. The dugong lives in the southwest Pacific Ocean, one species of manatee lives near the Amazon River, another around the West Indies, and a third off the coast of West Africa. These bulky animals grow 3–4 m long. Sea cows bobbing half-seen through ocean mists may have given rise to sailors' legends about mermaids (magical women with fish tails).

◪ The crabeater seal has few enemies, apart from killer whales and its larger cousin, the leopard seal.

SEA LIONS AND SEALS (pinnipeds)	Eared seals (fur seals and sea lions)
• 34 species	• 14 species
• smooth, streamlined head and bulky body	• ear flaps (may be hidden in fur)
• paddle-like limbs	• can tuck rear flippers under body
• sharp teeth	• inshore waters of most seas and oceans, ice floes
True or earless seals	• include northern fur seal, Californian sea lion, Galapagos fur seal
• 19 species	
• no visible or external ear flaps	Walrus
• cannot tuck rear flippers under body	• 1 species
• inshore waters of all seas and oceans but less common in tropics	• long tusks
• include grey seal, common (harbour) seal, harp seal, northern elephant seal, leopard seal, Mediterranean monk seal	• Arctic and northern oceans
	Manatees and dugong (sea cows)
	• 4 species
	• plant eaters
	• include Amazonian manatee, West Indian manatee, West African manatee, dugong

GREAT WHALES

WHALES AND DOLPHINS ARE PERFECTLY
ADAPTED TO LIFE AT SEA. In fact, they never come
ashore – unless beached by accident, when they usually
die. Great whales differ from toothed whales such as
dolphins and porpoises (page 132) because they have
comb-like baleen in their mouths, for filter-feeding. Great
whales were once hunted in huge numbers for their meat,
fat, oil and baleen (whalebone). The slaughter drove some
species almost to extinction. Laws now prevent
them from being killed in large numbers,
and most whale populations are
slowly recovering. Great whales
show complicated behaviour and
communicate with a wide
variety of sounds and calls.

(page 132)

> ### World Watch
> For centuries, small
> numbers of great whales
> were hunted with spear-like
> harpoons from sailing or
> rowing boats. But in the 19th
> century, whaling ships were
> equipped with steam
> engines. Then came faster
> diesel engines and explosive
> harpoons. The whales could
> not escape. Thousands were
> killed yearly. By the 1950s
> their numbers had
> plummeted. In the mid
> 1980s mass whaling ceased
> at last.

▲ Blue whale

Baleen whales have huge and very unusual
mouths. Their jaws lack teeth. Instead, the mouth
contains rows of baleen plates. These are strap-
like or curtain-like structures that hang down
from the roof of the mouth. They have fringed
edges like brushes or combs. They work as filters
to sieve the small animals of the plankton from the water.

▶ Humpback
whales open
their vast
mouths and
swim up to
the surface,
trapping
small
creatures
inside.

HOW GREAT WHALES FEED
These vast animals feed in
different ways. Right
whales cruise along with
their mouths open at
the surface. Blue and
humpback whales
take a massive
mouthful of sea
water, then press the huge tongue
upwards inside the mouth to force the
water out through the baleen plates.
The grey whale grubs in the mud of
the sea bed and does the same.
In all of these whales, food
items such as krill and small
fish get trapped in the
combs or bristles of the
baleen, which are tough
and springy, like
plastic. The whale
then licks the food
off the baleen
plates and
swallows it.

⬛ The grey whale feeds on small creatures in the mud, leaving great holes and furrows in the sea bed.

Grey whales feed mainly in the shallow coastal waters of the Arctic, between North America and Asia. They dive down to 90 m, scoop up a rich mixture of mud and filter the small animals living in it. When the whale has a mouthful of food it surfaces to strain off the water, swallows its meal and dives for another load.

⬛ Over millions of years of evolution, a whale's front legs have become flippers, used for swimming slowly and steering in the water. The rear legs have disappeared, while the tail has developed wide flukes. These swish up and down to drive the mammal through the water with the power of a racing car engine.

Most whales feed and travel in loose groups called pods. Members keep in touch using an amazing variety of sounds, many too low or high for us to hear. Blue and fin whales emit ear-splitting, low-pitched grunts that are the loudest noises made by any animal. Such sounds travel for hundreds of kilometres through the seas.

made by grey whales in the eastern Pacific. They travel each year from the breeding lagoons off the Californian and Mexican coasts to feed in the rich waters of the Bering Sea, and then back again – a distance of some 15,000 km. Humpbacks are also great travellers. Some spend the winter in the Caribbean and the summer near Greenland and Iceland.

LARGEST EVER... !
The largest animal that ever lived on Earth is the blue whale. An adult female blue whale can measure more than 30 m long, weigh over 150 tonnes and eat 4 tonnes of krill each day.

THE SONG OF THE HUMPBACK WHALE
Even more extraordinary are the songs of the humpback whale. These eerie, plaintive sounds plunge from high squeaks to deep wails, in a sequence that lasts half an hour or more, making it the longest, most complicated song of any animal. Usually, the singer is a male trying to attract a female at breeding time. Humpbacks also make acrobatic leaps almost right out of the water, then splash back in with an enormous crash.

Great whale calves stay with their mothers for up to a year. Like all mammals, they feed at first on her rich milk, but gradually they learn to filter-feed for themselves. A newborn blue whale calf weighs 3 tonnes and measures 7 m long. Each day it drinks 200 litres of milk. Female great whales usually have only one calf every two years – one reason why their numbers take so long to recover.

⬛ Minke whales are the smallest great whales, at 10–11 m in length.

WHALE MIGRATIONS
Many whales travel or migrate long distances between their main feeding places and the waters where the females give birth to their young, known as calves. Most great whales tend to feed in polar waters during the brief Arctic or Antarctic summer, then return near to the tropics for winter. The longest migrations are

DOLPHINS AND WHALES *(Cetaceans)*

- 76 species
- entirely aquatic, most in the sea
- long, submarine-shaped body
- front limbs are flippers
- tail flukes

The largest whales:

Baleen or great whales
- 10 species
- comb-like baleen in mouth
- worldwide, mainly colder oceans

Rorquals
- 6 species including blue whale (largest living animal), fin whale, humpback whale, minke whale, sei whale, Bryde's whale

Grey whale
- 1 species

Right whales
- 3 species including right whale, pygmy right whale, and bowhead

DOLPHINS AND PORPOISES

TOOTHED WHALES INCLUDE MANY KINDS OF PORPOISES AND DOLPHINS, AND ALSO SPERM WHALES, BEAKED WHALES AND TWO WHITE WHALES – THE NARWHAL AND BELUGA. These all have more normal mouths and teeth than great whales (page 130). However, unlike land carnivores, a toothed whale's teeth are all similar in size and shape, designed to grasp slippery fish and squid. The largest species of toothed whale is the sperm whale. Males or bulls are up to 20 m long and weigh 50 tonnes – making them the largest carnivores on Earth.

(page 130)

ON GUARD!

The narwhal grows to 5 m long and has mottled brown colouring. It also has a long tusk! Only the male has a tusk – a greatly lengthened upper left incisor tooth with a twisted spiral surface pattern. It grows up to 2.5 m long. Rival males "fence" with their tusks at breeding time.

☑ The common or harbour porpoise finds its prey of fish, such as herring or mackerel, using a sonar system of sound clicks and listening to the echoes.

Dolphins range in length from only 1.2 m in Heaviside's dolphin to 7 m or more in the huge and powerful killer whale, or orca. Killer whales are among the fiercest predators of the sea, though they rarely pose a threat to people. With immense speed and power, they pursue their prey of fish, seals, seabirds, dolphins and even larger whales. They hunt in groups and sometimes work together to herd a school of fish into shallow water to feed at their leisure.

☑ Narwhal

Like the other dolphins, killer whales are regarded as "intelligent" animals. This is partly because they can be taught to do tricks. But in the wild they also show great curiosity and

◁ The killer whale is the largest dolphin. It feeds mainly on seals and other sea mammals, as well as penguins and fish. It is a very fast swimmer, reaching a speed of 55 km/h.

adaptable behaviour, working out how to eat new and unfamiliar foods.

All of the dolphins are active, even playful creatures. They are sleek, powerful swimmers, and sometimes follow ships – perhaps to feast on any leftovers thrown over the side, or to save energy by swimming in the ship's wake. Most dolphins live in groups and communicate with each other using a great variety of squeals, buzzes, clicks and grunts. They also use these sounds for echolocation or sonar, like bats (page 106) but underwater, to find prey and navigate through cloudy water. Like all whales, they breathe through their nostrils, which are joined together on the top of the head as the blowhole.

(page 106)

SNUB-NOSED WHALES

☑ River dolphin

A dolphin has a protruding beak-like snout and a curving sickle-shaped back fin. Porpoises are similar, but lack the dolphin's beak and have a snub nose instead. They are also generally smaller than dolphins, growing to about 2 m in length. Most species are dark grey and feed, like dolphins, on fish and squid.

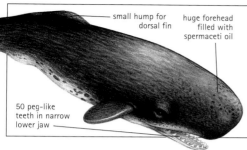

small hump for dorsal fin

huge forehead filled with spermaceti oil

50 peg-like teeth in narrow lower jaw

GIANT CARNIVORE

The massive sperm whale is the largest predator on the planet, and also the deepest-diving of all mammals. It reaches depths of 3 km in search of its prey, which includes the fearsome giant squid.

Porpoises tend to stay inshore, usually in small groups of about 10 or 15, and seldom leap clear of the water.

BIGGEST TOOTHED WHALES

Sperm whales feed mainly on large squid, which they catch deep in the ocean. The sperm whale is gigantic, but the dwarf sperm whale is more dolphin-sized, at about 2.6 m long. These whales are named for the waxy, oily substance, spermaceti, that takes up most of their bulging foreheads. It may help the whale to dive very deep and also to focus the sound waves it uses for echo-location.

BEAKED WHALES

The beaked whales are mysterious creatures that resemble overgrown dolphins. There are 18 species, but they spend most of their time diving to immense depths and

⬛ The northern bottlenose whale is a toothed whale— but it only has two teeth. These are in the lower jaw, and they may never grow above the gum.

so are seen much less often than other whales. They eat mainly squid. The largest is Baird's beaked whale, at about 13 m long.

The two kinds of white whales are the narwhal and beluga. The narwhal's sword-like tusk may have inspired legends about the mythical unicorn. The beluga is tuskless and is pure white when adult. It also has a flexible neck, so it can turn its head to each side. Belugas live in all Arctic and northern seas. They make such loud chirps, trills and squeaks that these can be heard above the water, earning them the nickname of "sea canary".

River dolphins live in fresh water and estuaries. Their echo-location is very sensitive, helping them find their way in muddy water. They include the very rare whitefin dolphin. There are perhaps only 150–200 left, in the Yangtze river in China.

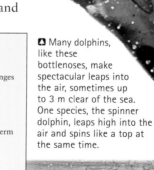

DOLPHINS AND WHALES
(continued from page 131):

Dolphins and other toothed whales
• 66 species
• mostly smaller than great whales
• short, sharp teeth

Groups include:

Dolphins
• 32 species
• worldwide, mainly offshore in warm seas
• beak-like snout
• includes common, bottlenose and spinner dolphins, melon-headed whale, pilot whales, killer whale (orca)

Porpoises
• 6 species
• northern coastal waters
• lack dolphin's "beak"
• includes common and Dall's porpoises

River dolphins
• 5 species
• fresh water
• Amazon, La Plata, Indus, Ganges and whitefin dolphins

Sperm whales
• 3 species
• blunt forehead
• includes sperm and pygmy sperm whales

Beaked whales
• 18 species
• resemble large dolphins with beak-like snout
• includes northern bottlenose whale and Cuvier's beaked whale

White whales
• 2 species
• whitish colour
• narwhal and beluga

⬛ Many dolphins, like these bottlenoses, make spectacular leaps into the air, sometimes up to 3 m clear of the sea. One species, the spinner dolphin, leaps high into the air and spins like a top at the same time.

ORANGS AND GORILLAS

THE ORANG, GORILLA, CHIMP AND PYGMY CHIMP ARE THE FOUR KINDS OF GREAT APES, AND THE LARGEST OF THE PRIMATES. They are also the closest living relatives of ourselves, the human species. The mysterious orangs live deep in the forests of Borneo and Sumatra, in Southeast Asia. They are difficult to spot because they are rare, very shy and live mainly on their own rather than in family groups or troops. Gorillas, the largest apes, dwell in a few restricted areas of West and Central Africa. They live in small groups. They are massive, muscular and powerful animals, yet also peaceful and gentle – unless threatened.

The name "orang-utan" means "man of the woods". This second-largest ape has bright reddish-brown fur, which is long and shaggy. Despite their size and weight, orangs are skilled at clambering around in the trees, spreading their weight using all four limbs. They are very fond of fruit and spend many hours feasting on a tree of ripe figs or mangoes. They also eat leaves and shoots. Their big teeth and strong jaws help them to tear open even hard nuts, and pull off strips of bark to get at the sap-laden soft wood beneath. Orangs also eat insects and the occasional egg, chick, small bird, lizard or mouse.

⬆ The female gorilla is pregnant for just over nine months. When the baby is born, it cannot walk or climb, but only cling to her fur. By about three months of age the youngster is sitting up, and by six months old, it is able to climb and walk. The mother feeds it on her milk for up to 18 months.

World Watch

Gorillas are the largest primates. A mature male is 1.8 m tall and weighs over 150 kg. But their size and power have not helped them survive. Rather, it has partly led to their plight. Gorillas have been shot for "sport". Their hands and feet are cut off for "trophies". They are among the most endangered of all animals, especially the mountain gorilla. Human conflicts where they live have not helped.

LARGEST... !

The orang-utan is the largest tree-living mammal. Males grow to 1.5 m tall and weigh 90 kg.

⬆ The massive head, neck, shoulders and arms of the gorilla make it the strongest primate. Large males weigh up to 180 kg.

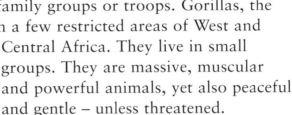

Gorillas usually sleep in nests that they make by bending and interlocking twigs and branches. Babies sleep with their mothers up to the age of about three years. These are mountain gorillas, with longer fur than the two lowland varieties.

The lowland gorillas have shorter, less shaggy fur than the rarer mountain gorillas.

THE LONG CALL

Orangs live in similar lowland rainforest habitats to gibbons. And like gibbons, orangs make loud calls to communicate with each other. However, it is only the male orang that does this, uttering what is known as his "long call", which lasts for a minute or two. The call starts with a series of roars, getting louder, then dying away to end with bubbling sounds. The call is not to keep in touch with family members, since orangs live solitary lives, except for a mother with her baby. The male probably makes the call to attract a female or to warn rival males off his territory.

Gorillas are very heavily built, with a broad chest, long arms and a large, tall-domed head (especially in adult males) with massive jaws and teeth. The nose is black, leathery and flattened. The fur and skin is mostly black, except in older adult males, which develop a silvery-white patch on the back and flanks, giving them the name of silverbacks.

platforms where they sleep at night. Younger gorillas spend part of the day in trees too. They weigh much less than the adults and so find climbing easier – and there are more branches that will bear their weight. But most older members of the gorilla group prefer to feed and travel on the ground. They amble along on all fours, using the soles of the feet and the bent knuckles of their hands.

Gorillas live in groups of about 5 to 35 animals. A typical group consists of one silverback male, one or two junior males, and several females with their offspring. Unlike most other monkeys and apes, gorillas are mostly silent, except when rival adult males meet. Then they may threaten each other. They beat their chests, thrash branches and make barking, roaring and hooting calls.

Orangs seem to make no distinction between their arms and legs, using all of them for both climbing and feeding.

THE MOST VEGETARIAN APE

Gorillas are strong and muscular enough to overpower any animal in their dense forest habitat. Yet they are almost entirely vegetarian. They feed mainly on leaves, shoots, stems and ferns, and occasionally ripe fruits. Their main feeding periods are early morning and mid-afternoon, with long rests in between.

In the early evening, gorillas climb into trees to weave nest

Old female orangs such as this one are smaller and lighter than old males. Old males develop long, shaggy fur, especially over the shoulders and back, and loose, wrinkled skin on the chest and belly.

SOME GROUPS OF APES (the great apes):

Great apes
• 4 species
• largest primates
• tailless
• fingers and thumb can manipulate small items

Gorilla
• 2 species
• Western gorilla (Gorilla gorilla)
• Eastern gorilla (Gorilla beringei)
• 3 varieties or subspecies:

Western lowland gorilla (Cameroon, Central African Republic, Congo, Gabon, Equatorial Guinea)
Eastern lowland gorilla (eastern Congo)
Mountain gorilla (Congo, Rwanda, Uganda)
• eats plant material, berries, fruits

Orang (orang-utan)
• 2 species
• Bornean orang-utan (Pongo pygmaeus)
• Sumatran orang-utan (Pongo abelii)

CHIMPANZEES

CHIMPANZEES HAVE THE MOST COMPLICATED SOCIAL LIVES OF ALL THE APES. They have a huge range of facial expressions, body postures, gestures, signs and sounds. They can work out how to solve simple problems, in the wild and in captivity. They make and use simple tools. In many ways, they seem to be a link between the world of animals and our human world. Their body structure and genes, their behaviour and intelligence, and their evolution as shown by fossils, mean that chimps are our closest relatives.

A mother chimp cares for her youngster for up to three years.

The pygmy chimp, or bonobo, is only slightly smaller than the common chimp, with a head–body length of 55–65 cm.

There are two species of chimpanzee. These are the chimp or common chimpanzee, and the bonobo or pygmy chimpanzee. The chimp is covered with black or grey hair, except for the ears, face, hands and feet. The face is usually pink, turning darker brown or black with age. The pygmy chimp is slightly smaller, with a lighter build and smaller teeth, and a darker face. It also has sideways tufts of hair over its ears.

Both species of chimps are long-lived. Some reach 50 years of age. More than any other animals, they show degrees of human-like attributes. These include care for their kin, teamwork during hunting, sharing out food, long-lasting bonds or "friendships", the ability to learn through their lives as they acquire skills, use tools and work out problems, with a good long-term memory for individuals, places and events. A chimp also shows self-awareness. Unlike other animals, it recognizes that the reflection in a mirror is itself, not another chimp.

THE TWO CHIMPS

There are several differences between the common chimp and the pygmy chimp. But these are quite minor, even in overall size. Some experts suggest that the two chimps are really varieties, or subspecies, of the same species.

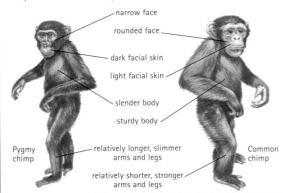

narrow face
rounded face
dark facial skin
light facial skin
slender body
sturdy body
Pygmy chimp
relatively longer, slimmer arms and legs
Common chimp
relatively shorter, stronger arms and legs

However, chimps can also show aggression and violence that is not directed towards catching food or in self-defence against rivals, as it is in other animals. In humans, this type of aggression might be described as "mindless".

THE CHIMP'S DAY

Chimpanzees are mainly active during the day. They rise at dawn to search for food, and spend time feeding and resting.

Chimps spend many hours grooming others in their family or group. They remove old hairs, bits of dirt and pests such as fleas from each other's fur and skin. Apart from improving hygiene, this mutual grooming helps to strengthen the relationships within the troop.

MAKING FACES

Chimpanzees use a kind of language to tell each other important information about their surroundings and intentions. They use many facial expressions and utter various shouts and grunts. Tame chimps have learned our own sign language, using their hands to communicate with people.

thoughtful

pleased

angry

When they move on, they travel (like gorillas) mainly on the ground rather than in trees, knuckle-walking on all fours. At night, each adult makes itself a nest platform, like the gorilla's. The chimp bends and weaves together branches, twigs and leaves, and rests and sleeps until the morning.

THE CHIMP'S HABITAT

Ideal chimp habitat includes areas with fruit trees, since fruit is their major food and they eat it for at least 4–5 hours each day. Other favoured foods are young, freshly sprouted leaves, seeds and also soft bark, sap, juicy pith wood and flowers. They sometimes use rocks to smash open hard-cased fruits and nuts, such as those of oil palms.

Chimps also eat termites, ants and caterpillars. A chimp may use a stick to probe inside a termite mound. The insects crawl onto the twig, and the chimp pulls it out and licks them off. Groups of chimps occasionally work together to catch and eat young pigs, monkeys and antelopes.

An adult male chimp is far stronger than an adult human, with a broad chest and very muscular arms. Male chimps, especially, get into fights or territorial disputes. They pick up and hurl large boulders or branches with great ease. Most chimp troops number about 20–50 individuals, with one or two large, leading males, various younger males and the rest females with their young.

Chimp numbers have fallen rapidly in recent years. The main causes are habitat destruction and illegal trapping. Many of the remaining populations are small and separated, and so at risk of extinction.

APES (continued from page 135):

Chimpanzees
• 2 species

Common chimpanzee
• West and Central Africa, from Senegal to Tanzania, mainly in Congo, Gabon, Cameroon
• forest, patchy woodland
• fruits, seeds, soft bark and other plant parts, also insects, eggs, small mammals

Pygmy chimpanzee (bonobo)
• Central Africa, only in Congo
• rainforest
• fruits, shoots, leaves, buds

▶ Many facial expressions made by chimps look similar to our own. However, we must be very careful about assuming that a chimp's expression that looks like our own, means the same as our version. A chimp who appears to be in a good mood and laughing (right) is really fearful, baring its teeth in defence to a threat. Chimps learn much during their long "childhood".

137

GLOSSARY

Abdomen The region of an animal's body that contains mainly the parts or organs for digestion, reproduction and excretion (getting rid of waste products).

Antenna A "feeler", a long and thin part, usually on or near the head, that detects touch – and perhaps smells and tastes as well.

Arthropod An invertebrate animal that has a hard outer body casing (exoskeleton) and jointed limbs, such as an insect, crab, spider, centipede or millipede.

Asexual reproduction Producing offspring without sex (see Sexual reproduction). For example, some simple animals simply split in two (fission). Some grow "buds" that detach to form new individuals (vegetative reproduction). Some female animals produce eggs that develop into young without being fertilized by the sperm from a male (parthenogenesis).

Camouflage When an animal is shaped, coloured and patterned to blend in with its surroundings, so that it is less likely to be noticed, especially by its predators or prey.

Canine teeth Long, sharp teeth, like spears or daggers, near the front of the mouth of a mammal. They are well developed in meat-eaters such as dogs and cats.

Carapace A large, hard, shield-like covering over an animal's body. The upper part of the shell of a turtle is a carapace. So is the top part of the shell of a crab.

Carnivore An animal that eats the meat or flesh of other animals. Most carnivores are predators.

Carrion "Dead meat" — the dead and dying bodies or carcasses of animals, which are usually eaten by scavengers.

Cilia Microscopic hair-like parts that coat many outer surfaces and inner linings of animals and their body parts, such as the body surface of a tiny worm or the inside of the intestine. Cilia wave to-and-fro like tiny oars to cause movement.

Compound eye An eye made up of many separate light-detecting units, like a mosaic, rather than one larger unit, like our own eye. Insects have compound eyes.

Courtship behaviour The movements, actions, sounds and scents made by a male and/or female animal of the same species, when they come together to mate.

Detritivore An animal that feeds on detritus – the dead, dying and rotting bits of animals, plants and other once-living things.

Digestion Breaking down bits of food into tiny pieces by squeezing and squashing them, and pouring powerful chemical juices onto them. The pieces or nutrients are small enough to be taken into body tissues for growth and life processes.

Digit A toe, finger or similar part on the end of a limb.

Dorsal On the top, upper side or back of an animal, like a fish's dorsal fin.

Echo-location A system of sending out sounds, listening to the echoes that bounce back and working out the position of nearby objects. Bats, dolphins, shrews and some birds use echo-location.

Egg A single living cell produced by a female animal for reproduction. Some eggs are microscopic. Birds' eggs are large and enclosed in a hard shell.

Endoskeleton A strong supporting framework on the inside of the body, such as our own bones.

Evolution The changes in living things through time, due to changing conditions. New species appear, and existing species that are not suited or adapted to the conditions, and which cannot change or evolve, die out or become extinct.

Exoskeleton A strong supporting framework on the outside of the body, such as an insect's body casing.

Extinction When all the members of a particular group of living thing, usually a species, die out so that the species disappears forever.

Eye A body part that detects light rays and produces nerve signals that go to the animal's brain. (See also Compound eye.)

Filter-feeding When an animal feeds by filtering or sieving lots of tiny particles, usually from water, using body parts shaped like combs, brushes or feathers.

Flagellum A long, whip-like part sticking out from a microscopic cell. It lashes to-and-fro to cause movement.

Food chain and web The links between different living things, according to how they obtain their food. A simple food chain is when a rabbit eats some grass, and a fox eats the rabbit:
Grass > Rabbit > Fox
In nature, many animals eat a variety of foods, so the food chains link into a complex network known as a food web.

Genes Instructions or blueprints to make living things, in the form of chemical codes of the substance DNA (deoxyribonucleic acid), found inside cells. A living thing develops in shape, size and colour, and carries out its digestion and other body processes, according to the genes it is born with.

Gills Body parts specialized for absorbing oxygen dissolved in water. They are usually delicate and feathery.

Gland A body part that makes a certain product, usually a liquid, for use by the animal. A salivary gland, for example, makes saliva (spit), a venom gland makes poison and a mucus gland makes slimy mucus.

Habitat A type of natural place with characteristic plants and animals, such as a pond, an oak wood or a rocky seashore. Some animals, such as penguins, live only in one habitat. Others, such as the red fox, range across many habitats.

Herbivore An animal that eats mainly plants or their parts and products, such as leaves, fruits or roots.

Hermaphrodite An animal that has both female and male sex organs, which allow it to produce both eggs and sperm for reproduction.

Hibernation When a warm-blooded animal goes into a "deep sleep" during adverse conditions. Its body temperature falls drastically and its heartbeat, breathing and other body processes almost stop.

Incisor tooth Long, sharp-edged, chisel-like teeth at the front of the mouth of a mammal. They are well developed in rodents (gnawing animals) such as mice, rats and beavers.

Insectivore An animal that eats mainly insects, especially ants or termites, and often other small prey items too, such as worms, spiders, slugs and snails.

Invertebrate An animal without a backbone, or more accurately, without a vertebral column (see Vertebrate). The vast majority of animals, both in numbers of individuals and numbers of species, are invertebrates (eg insects, starfish and worms).

Kingdom One of the five main groups of living things. Animals make up the biggest kingdom, Animalia.

Larva The active growing and feeding stage in the lives of certain animals. It usually follows the egg stage. A larva does not look like its parent.

Lungs Body parts specialized for absorbing oxygen from air.

Metamorphosis When an animal changes its body shape dramatically as it grows. For example, a butterfly begins life as an egg, hatches into a caterpillar (larva), then turns into a chrysalis (pupa), and finally into the adult butterfly.

Migration A long journey to find food or more suitable conditions. Some migrations are regular, to-and-fro along the same route, at the same time each year. Others are occasional, as when lemmings run out of food and set off in almost any direction.

Molar teeth Wide, flat teeth at the back of the mouth of a mammal, for chewing. They are well developed in herbivores such as zebras, antelopes and elephants.

Mucus A slimy, usually sticky substance made by many animals, for uses such as protection, trapping bits of food, deterring enemies or easing movement.
Muscle A body part of an animal specialized to get shorter, or contract. Muscles make movements.

New World Term used for the continents and nearby islands of North and South America. They are separated from the Old World by the Atlantic and Pacific Oceans.

Nutrients Substances such as minerals that a living thing takes in as food, so it can grow, maintain and repair its body, and use energy for life processes.

Old World Term used for the continents and main islands of Europe,

Africa, Asia and Australia. They are separated from the New World by the Atlantic and Pacific Oceans.

Omnivore An animal that eats many kinds of food, including meat and plants.

Oxygen An invisible gas, with no taste or smell, that makes up one fifth of the air around us. Oxygen is needed by living things because it is a vital part of the chemical process that breaks down food to get energy. Most animals obtain oxygen through their gills or lungs, or by absorbing it through the body's surface.

Parasite A living thing that exists on or in another living thing, known as the host. The parasite gains something, such as shelter or food, and usually causes harm to the host it lives on.

Parthenogenesis See Asexual reproduction.

Pheromone A chemical substance, like a scent, that an animal releases into the air or spreads on the ground. Each pheromone causes a certain reaction in others of its species, such as getting ready to breed, or following the pheromone trail to food.

Predator An animal that hunts or actively pursues other, usually smaller, creatures – its prey — for food.

Prehensile A body part that is flexible and muscular, and which can be used for grasping and holding. Some monkeys have prehensile tails for gripping branches.

Prey Any animal that is pursued or hunted as food by a predator.

Proboscis A movable stalk-like part on the head of an animal, usually with the mouth on it or near it.

Pupa The seemingly inactive, resting stage in the lives of certain animals, such as insects. It usually follows the larva stage and is sometimes called a chrysalis or cocoon.

Sexual reproduction When a sperm cell joins with an egg cell to make a fertilized egg, which develops into a new individual. This usually involves a female and male of the same species mating (having sex). (See Asexual reproduction.)

Species A kind or type of living thing, such as the tiger, the golden eagle, the African elephant or the common octopus.

Members of a species can breed with each other, but not with members of another species.

Sperm A single living cell, usually shaped like a microscopic tadpole, produced by a male animal for reproduction. (See Sexual reproduction.)

Symbiosis When two different kinds or species of living things exist closely together and benefit each other in some way, such as giving protection to the other creature from potential predators, or sharing food. Sea anemones and clown fish have a symbiotic relationship. The fish's thick coating of slime protects it against the anemone's stings.

Territory An area that an animal occupies and defends against rivals of its species. Some territories are for feeding, some are for breeding and some are for both. A tiger's territory covers dozens of square kilometres of forest. A limpet's territory is just a few square metres of seashore rock.

Thorax The region of an animal's body that contains mainly the parts for moving, such as legs or wings, and often those for breathing and pumping blood (the heart). In the human body it is called the chest.

Torpor When a cold-blooded animal becomes inactive, usually because the temperature falls, as at night or in winter.

Vegetative reproduction See Asexual reproduction.

Ventral On the underside or belly of an animal, like a fish's ventral fin.

Vertebrate An animal with a backbone or, more accurately, a vertebral column – a row of bones or cartilages called vertebrae. The main groups of vertebrates are fish, amphibians, reptiles, birds and mammals.

Viviparous When a female animal gives birth to babies ("live young"), rather than laying eggs.

Warning colours Bright colours and patterns on an animal's body, which warn others that it is dangerous or harmful in some way. It may have a sting, or a poison bite, or a horrible taste. Red and black or yellow and black are common warning colours, found on bees, wasps, beetles, frogs, snakes and various other animals.

INDEX

A

accipiters 91
agamid lizards 78, 79
agrippa moths 45
albatrosses 86, 87
alligators 72, 76-77
alpacas 116
amoebas 12, 13
amphibians 68-71
anacondas 81
animal kingdom 6, 9
annelid worms 26, 27
anteaters 102, 108, 109
antelopes 116
apes 7, 134-137
arachnids 40, 41, 50-51
archerfish 64
arctic foxes 124
armadillos 108, 109
arthropods 40-51
    arachnids 40, 41, 50-51
    crustaceans 41, 48-49
    insects 40-47
asses 118
auks 86, 87
axolotls 69

B

babirusas 117
bacteria 6, 14
bald eagles 91
baleen whales 130
bandicoots 105
barn owls 95
basilisk lizards 78-79
bath sponges 17
bats 106-107
beaked whales 132, 133
bears 122, 126-127
beavers 114-115
bees 41
beetles 40, 42-43
belugas 132, 133
bird-eating spiders 50, 51
birds 7, 9, 84-99
    birds of prey 90-91
    flightless birds 84-85
    owls and nightjars 94-95
    perching birds 96-99
    pigeons, doves and parrots 92-93
    seabirds 86-87
    wading birds 88-89
    waterfowl 88-89
birds of paradise 97
bitterlings 59
bitterns 88, 89
bivalves 30, 31
blind snakes 80, 81
blue whales 130
boas 6, 80, 81
bobcats 123
bonobos 136
boobies 86, 87
boobooks 95
bowerbirds 96, 97
breeding 7
brimstone butterflies 44, 45
bristleworms 28-29
brittlestars 16, 37
bryozoans 14-15
budgerigars 92
bugs 40-41, 46
bulbuls 97
bullfrogs 69
buntings 98, 99
buteos 91
butterflies 44-45
buzzards 91

C

caecilians 69
caimans 73, 76, 77
camels 116
cane toads 71
capybaras 114
caracals 123
cardinals 98
caribou 116
carnivores 7, 122-127
carp 58-59
cassowaries 84, 85
caterpillars 7, 44
catfish 58, 59
cats 122-123
cats, domestic 123
cattle 116
cavies 112, 115
centipedes 40, 41
cephalopods 30, 34-35
chaffinches 98
chameleons 78, 79
characins 58, 59
cheetahs 122
chelonians 74-75
chimaeras 54, 55, 56-57
chimpanzees 134, 136-137
chinchillas 114, 115
chitons 31
ciliates 12-13
civets 122
clams 30, 31
classification system 9
clearwings 44
clown fish 21
cnidarians 22
cockatoos 93
cockles 30, 31
cockroaches 8, 40, 46
colugos 105
conches 31
condors 90, 91
corals 16, 22-23
cormorants 86, 87
corn buntings 99
cougars 123
cowfish 63
coyotes 124
coypus 114, 115
crabeater seals 128, 129
crabs 20, 21, 40, 41, 48-49
cranes 88
crayfish 41, 48-49
crickets 41, 46-47
croakers 64, 65
crocodiles 72, 73, 76-77
crossbills 98
crown-of-thorns starfish 37
crows 96
crustaceans 41, 48-49
cuttlefish 30, 35

D

darters 65
Darwin, Charles 75
deer 116, 117
detritivores 7
dingoes 125
diving beetles 42, 43
dodos 84
dogfish 55
dogs 122, 124-125
dogs, domestic 125
dolphins 132-133
dormice 112, 113
doves 92-93

dragonflies 46
dromedaries 116
drum fish 64, 65
ducks 88, 89
dugongs 129
dung beetles 41, 43

E
eagle owls 94, 95
eagles 90, 91
earthworms 26-27
earwigs 46
echidnas 102, 103
echinoderms 36-37
echlocation 95, 106-107, 132
egg-laying mammals 102-103
egrets 88
electric eels 59
elephant birds 85
elephants 120-121
elf owls 94
elk 117
emus 84, 85
endangered species 8
entoprocts 15
equids 118-119
euglenas 13
evolution 6, 9
extinction 8

F
falcons 90, 91
fanworms 26, 28
feather stars 36, 37
fennec foxes 124
finches 98, 99
fireflies 43
fish 7, 54-65
    bony fish 54, 55
    cartilaginous fish 54, 55, 56-57
    jawless fish 54, 55
fish eagles 90
fishing owls 95
flamingoes 88
flatfish 62-63
flounders 62
flying dragons 79
flying foxes 107
flying frogs 71
foxes 124-125
frigate birds 86, 87
frilled lizards 79
frogmouths 94, 95

frogs 7, 8, 68, 69, 70-71
fruit flies 41
furniture beetles 43

G
gannets 86, 87
garden snails 32
gastropods 30, 32
geckoes 72
geese 88-89
genets 122
gerbils 112
gharials 76, 77
giant ram's-horn snails 33
giraffes 116, 117
glassfish 59
gliders 105
glow worms 43
golden eagles 90, 91
goldfinches 98
goldfish 58
goliath beetles 43
gorillas 134, 135
goshawks 91
grasshoppers 8, 41, 46-47
great horned owls 95
grizzly bears 127
groupers 64-65
guanacos 116
guillemots 87
guinea pigs 112
gulls 8, 86, 87
gurnards 61
gyrfalcons 90

H
habitats and habitat destruction 8, 9
hagfish 9, 54, 55
halibut 62, 63
hamsters 112, 113
hares 110-111
harp seals 129
harvest mice 112
harvestmen 50
hawfinches 98, 99
hawkfish 55
hawkmoths 45
hawks 90, 91
herbivores 7
hermaphrodites 27, 32
hermit crabs 20, 21, 48
herons 88, 89
hippopotamuses 116, 117

hobbies 90, 91
honey possums 105
horned owls 9
hornwrack 15
horses 118-119
humpback whales 130, 131
huntsman spiders 50
hyenas 122, 124-125

I
ibises 88, 89
iguanas 73, 78-79
insects 40-47
    beetles and weevils 42-43
    butterflies and moths 44-45
    crickets and grasshoppers 46-47
invertebrates 9

J
jackals 124, 125
jackdaws 96
jackrabbits 111
jaguars 123
jays 96, 97
jellyfish 7, 18-19
jerboas 112, 113
jewfish 64
Johnston's crocodiles 77
jumping mice 113

K
kakapos 84, 85
kangaroos 104, 105
kestrels 91
killer whales 132
kinkajous 127
kites 91
kiwis 84, 85
knifefish 59
koalas 104, 105
krill 48, 49

L
lagomorphs 110
lammergeiers 91
lampreys 54, 55
leaf insects 46-47
leeches 26-27
lemmings 112, 113
lemurs 105
leopard seals 129
leopards 123
Lepidoptera 44-45

limpets 30, 32
lionfish 60
lions 8, 122, 123
lion's mane jellyfish 18
little owls 95
lizards 72, 73, 78-79
llamas 116, 117
lobsters 40, 48-49
locusts 40, 46
lories 93
lorikeets 93
lovebirds 93
lugworms 26, 28, 29
lumpsuckers 60
lynxes 122, 123
lyrebirds 96, 97

M
macaws 93
magpies 96
malaria 12, 13
mammals 7, 102-137
    anteaters, sloths and armadillos 108-109
    bats 106-107
    carnivores 122-133
    egg-laying mammals 102-103
    elephants 120-121
    marsupials 104-105
    primates 134-137
    rabbits, hares and pikas 110-111
    rodents 112-115
    ungulates 116-119
    whales, dolphins and porpoises 130-133
manatees 128, 129
mantids 46, 47
maras 115
margays 123
marsupials 104-105
matamatas 74, 75
metamorphosis 44, 45, 46
mice 8, 112-113
millipedes 40, 41
minke whales 131
minotaur beetles 43
mites 41, 50
moas 85
mockingbirds 97
mole rats 113
moles 104, 105
molluscs 30-35
    bivalves 30, 31
    cephalopods 30, 34-35
    gastropods 30, 32-33

mongooses 122
monk seals 129
monkfish 54
monotremes 102-103
moon jellyfish (aurelia) 19
mosquitoes 8, 12, 13, 40
moss animals 14-15
moths 44-45
Murray cod 65
mussels 7, 30, 31, 59
mynahs 97

N
narwhals 132, 133
nautiluses 30, 34, 35
neon tetras 59
net-casting spiders 51
newts 68-69
nightjars 94-95
Nile crocodiles 76, 77
Nile perch 54, 64
nudibranchs 33

O
ocelots 122, 123
octopuses 30, 31, 34-35
oilbirds 95
omnivores 7
opossums 104
orangutans 134-135
orioles 97
orthopterans 46-47
osprey 90, 91
ostriches 84, 85
owls 9, 94-95
oysters 30

P
Pacific blue stars 37
pampas cats 123
pandas 122, 126-127
pangolins 108, 109
parakeets 92, 93
parasites 12, 13, 27
parrots 84, 85, 92-93
parthenogenesis 47
passerines 96-99
peacock worms 28
peccaries 116, 117
penguins 8, 84, 85
perch 54, 64-65
peregrine falcons 90
petrels 86, 87

pigeons 92-93
pigs 116, 117
pikas 110, 111
pipe snakes 80, 81
pipefish 60, 61
pipistrelles 106, 107
piranhas 59
placozoans 17
plaice 62, 63
plankton 19, 23
platypuses 102-103
poison-arrow frogs 71
polar bears 127
polyps 16, 22-23
porcupinefish 62, 63
porcupines 114, 115
porpoises 132-133
possums 105
potoos 94
prawns 49
praying mantis 47
primates 134-137
protists 6, 12-13, 14
protozoans 12
Przewalski's horse 118
pufferfish 62
puffins 7, 87
pythons 73, 80-81

Q
queleas 98

R
rabbits 110-111
raccoons 122, 126-127
ragworms 26, 28
rails 88
raptors 90-91
ratfish 56, 57
ratites 84, 85
rats 8, 112-113
ravens 96
rays 54, 55, 56-57, 62
razorbills 87
razorshells 30, 31
reef sharks 57
reindeer 116
reptiles 9, 72-81
    crocodiles and alligators 72, 73, 76-77
    lizards 72, 73, 78-79
    snakes 72, 73, 80-81
    turtles, tortoises and terrapins 74-75
rheas 84, 85

rhinoceros beetles 42
rhinoceroses 118, 119
rodents 112-115
rooks 96

S
salamanders 68-69
saltwater crocodiles 72, 76
sand stars 37
scallops 30
scarab beetles 43
scorpionfish 60, 61
scorpions 40, 41, 50
sea anemones 20-21
sea cows 129
sea cucumbers 36
sea fans 22
sea lilies 36, 37
sea lions 122, 128, 129
sea mat 15
sea mosses 14-15
sea moths 60
sea mouse 29
sea slugs 30, 33
sea snails 32
sea urchins 36
seabass 64, 65
seabirds 86-87
seadragons 60
seahorses 60-61
seals 122, 128-129
secretary birds 91
sexton beetles 43
sharks 54, 55, 56-57
shearwaters 86, 87
short-eared owls 95
shrikes 96
shrimpfish 60
shrimps 8, 20, 40, 48, 49
skimmers 87
skinks 73
skuas 86, 87
slime mould 13
sloths 108, 109
sludge worms 27
slugs 30, 31, 32-33
snails 30, 31, 32-33
snakes 72, 73, 80-81
snapping turtles 74, 75
snow buntings 98
snow leopards 123
snowshoe hares 110
snowy owls 94

song thrushes 33
sparrowhawks 91
sparrows 98-99
sperm whales 132, 133
spider crabs 49
spiders 40, 41, 50-51
spiny anteaters 102
sponges 7, 16-17
spoonbills 89
squid 30, 31, 34-35
stalked jellyfish 18, 19
starfish 7, 36-37
starlings 97
stauromedusans 18
stick insects 46, 47
sticklebacks 60, 61
stinkbugs 8
stonefish 60
stoneflies 46
storks 88, 89
sun bears 126
sunbeam snakes 80
sunfish 62, 63
sunstar 20
Surinam toads 70, 71
swans 88, 89
symbiosis 20

T
tadpoles 7, 68, 69, 70
tapirs 118, 119
Tasmanian devils 104
termites 40, 46
terns 86-87
terrapins 72, 73, 74
thread snakes 80, 81
ticks 40, 50
tiger beetles 43
tigerfish 58
tigers 123
tinamous 85
toads 69, 70-71
tortoises 72, 73, 74-75
trapdoor spiders 50
tree frogs 70, 71
triggerfish 62-63
tropicbirds 87
trumpetfish 60
tuataras 6, 73
tubesnout 60
tubeworms 29
turtles 72, 73, 74-75
tusk shells 31

U
ungulates 116-119

V
vampire bats 106, 107
vertebrates 9, 54
vicunas 116
Virginia opossums 104
viscachas 115
vultures 90, 91

W
wallabies 104
walleyes 65
walruses 128, 129
warthogs 117
wasps 40
water dragons 73
water fleas 48
water and pond snails 32
water snakes 73
waxbills 98
weasels 122
weaver birds 98-99
weevils 42-43
whale sharks 57
whales 130-131
whelks 30, 32
whirligig beetles 43
whydahs 98
wild boar 117
wild dogs 122, 125
winkles 30
wolf spiders 51
wolves 122, 124, 125
wombats 104, 105
wood turtles 75
woodlice 48
worm lizards 73
worms 26-29

Z
zebras 118-119
zooids 14

ACKNOWLEDGEMENTS

The publishers wish to thank the following artists who have contributed to this publication:

Janet Baker (Julian Baker Illustrations), Andy Beckett (Illustration), John Butler, Kuo Kang Chen, Wayne Ford, Chris Forsey, Roger Gorringe (Illustration), Ron Hayward, Roger Kent (Illustration), Stuart Lafford (Linden Artists), Mick Loates (Linden Artists), Alan Male (Linden Artists), Matt Nicholas (David Lewis Agency), Jane Pickering (Linden Artists), Terry Riley, Mike Saunders, Sarah Smith (Linden Artists), Christian Webb (Temple Rogers), David Webb (Linden Artists), Martin Wilcock (Illustration).

The publishers wish to thank the following photographic sources for the use of their photographs in this publication:

OSF = Oxford Scientific Films; NHPA = Natural History Photographic Agency

Page 12-13 (C) Peter Parks/OSF; 14 (C/L) Harold Taylor/OSF; 15 (B/R) Karen Gowlett-Holmes/OSF; 18 (B) Frederik Ehrenstrom/OSF; 20 (B/L) Norbert Wu/NHPA; 23 (T/R) A.N.T./NHPA; 29 (T/L) David Fox/OSF, (B) Rodger Jackman/OSF; 31 (C/R) Peter Parks/OSF; 32 (T/L) Colin Milkins/OSF; 32 (T/R) Rudie H.Kuiter/OSF; 37 (T/L) Peter Parks/OSF; 43 (L/T) Kjell B. Sandved/OSF; 44 (B/R) London Scientific Films/OSF; 46 (B) Alastair Shay/OSF; 49 (C) Jan Aldenhoven/OSF; 51 (B/L) A.N.T./NHPA; 58 (B) D. Heuclin/NHPA; 61 (R) David B.Fleetham/OSF; 62-63 (C) NHPA; 64 (B) Tobias Bernhard/OSF; 64 (T/L) G.I. Bernard/NHPA; 70 (B/R) G.I. Bernard/NHPA; 70 (B/L) Stephen Dalton/NHPA; 73 (T/R) Martin Harvey/NHPA; 77 (T/L) Daniel Heuclin/NHPA; 78-79 (B) Stephen Dalton/NHPA; 79 (T/L) Stephen Dalton/NHPA; 81 (T/L) Jany Sauvanet/NHPA; 85 (R) Tui de Roy/OSF; 88-89 (B) David C. Fritts/Animals Animals/OSF; 92-93 (C) L. Hugh Newman/NHPA; 97 (B/R) Michael Morcombe/NHPA; 99 (B) Maurice Tibbs/Survival Anglia/OSF; 103 (R) A.N.T./NHPA; 106 (T/L) Richard la Val/Animals Animals/OSF; 107 (C) Stephen Dalton/NHPA; 109 (T/R) Michael Fogden/OSF; 111 (C/R) Manfred Danegger/NHPA; 112 (B/L) Andrew Thomson; 113 (C/L) Raymond A. Mendez/Animals Animals/OSF; 125 (T/L) Peter Pickford/NHPA; 129 (T/R) A.N.T./NHPA; 133 (B) Konrad Wothe/OSF; 135 (T/C) Martin Harvey/NHPA; 136 (C/R) Martyn Colbeck/OSF.